FIRST NAME

HOME ADDRESS (LINE 1)

HOME ADDRESS (LINE 2)

HOME PHONE   MOBILE PHONE

EMAIL

BUSINESS/COLLEGE ADDRESS (LINE 1)

BUSINESS/COLLEGE ADDRESS (LINE 2)

BUSINESS/COLLEGE PHONE   BUSINESS/COLLEGE EMAIL

EMERGENCY CONTACT (NAME AND PHONE NUMBER)

BLOOD GROUP

ALLERGIES

VACCINATIONS

UK BANK HOLIDAYS

JANUARY 1ST — New Year's Day

APRIL 18TH — Good Friday

APRIL 21ST — Easter Monday

MAY 5TH — Early May Bank Holiday

MAY 26TH — Spring Bank Holiday

AUGUST 25TH — Summer Bank Holiday

DECEMBER 25TH — Christmas Day

DECEMBER 26TH — Boxing Day

US FEDERAL HOLIDAYS

JANUARY 1ST — New Year's Day

JANUARY 20TH — Martin Luther King Jr. Day

FEBRUARY 17TH — Presidents' Day

MAY 26TH — Memorial Day

JUNE 19TH — Juneteenth

JULY 4TH — Independence Day

SEPTEMBER 1ST — Labor Day

OCTOBER 13TH — Indigenous Peoples' Day

NOVEMBER 11TH — Veterans Day

NOVEMBER 27TH — Thanksgiving

DECEMBER 25TH — Christmas Day

Verso Books is the largest independent,
radical publishing house in the English-speaking world.

Launched by *New Left Review* in 1970, Verso
is a leading publisher in current affairs, philosophy,
history, politics and economics.

"A rigorously intelligent publisher."
—*SUNDAY TIMES*

"Anglo-America's preeminent radical press."
—*HARPER'S*

VERSOBOOKS.COM

Buy securely and easily from our website—
great discounts, free shipping with a minimum order
and a free ebook bundled with many of our hard-copy books.

Check our website to read our blog and see our
latest titles—featuring essays, videos, podcasts,
interviews with authors, news, exclusive competitions
and details of forthcoming events.

Sign up to our email list to be the first to hear of
our new titles, special offers and events.

Verso Books   @VersoBooks   versobooks   versobooks

Some of the quotes in the calendar are drawn
from *The Verso Book of Dissent*, edited by
Andrew Hsiao and Audrea Lim (Verso 2020).

2025

JANUARY

S	M	T	W	TH	F	S
29	30	31	1	2	3	4
5	6	7	8	9	10	11
12	13	14	15	16	17	18
19	20	21	22	23	24	25
26	27	28	29	30	31	1

FEBRUARY

S	M	T	W	TH	F	S
26	27	28	29	30	31	1
2	3	4	5	6	7	8
9	10	11	12	13	14	15
16	17	18	19	20	21	22
23	24	25	26	27	28	1

MARCH

S	M	T	W	TH	F	S
23	24	25	26	27	28	1
2	3	4	5	6	7	8
9	10	11	12	13	14	15
16	17	18	19	20	21	22
23	24	25	26	27	28	29
30	31					

APRIL

S	M	T	W	TH	F	S
30	31	1	2	3	4	5
6	7	8	9	10	11	12
13	14	15	16	17	18	19
20	21	22	23	24	25	26
27	28	29	30	1	2	3

MAY

S	M	T	W	TH	F	S
27	28	29	30	1	2	3
4	5	6	7	8	9	10
11	12	13	14	15	16	17
18	19	20	21	22	23	24
25	26	27	28	29	30	31

JUNE

S	M	T	W	TH	F	S
1	2	3	4	5	6	7
8	9	10	11	12	13	14
15	16	17	18	19	20	21
22	23	24	25	26	27	28
29	30	1	2	3	4	5

JULY

S	M	T	W	TH	F	S
29	30	1	2	3	4	5
6	7	8	9	10	11	12
13	14	15	16	17	18	19
20	21	22	23	24	25	26
27	28	29	30	31	1	2

AUGUST

S	M	T	W	TH	F	S
27	28	29	30	31	1	2
3	4	5	6	7	8	9
10	11	12	13	14	15	16
17	18	19	20	21	22	23
24	25	26	27	28	29	30
31						

SEPTEMBER

S	M	T	W	TH	F	S
31	1	2	3	4	5	6
7	8	9	10	11	12	13
14	15	16	17	18	19	20
21	22	23	24	25	26	27
28	29	30	1	2	3	4

OCTOBER

S	M	T	W	TH	F	S
28	29	30	1	2	3	4
5	6	7	8	9	10	11
12	13	14	15	16	17	18
19	20	21	22	23	24	25
26	27	28	29	30	31	1

NOVEMBER

S	M	T	W	TH	F	S
26	27	28	29	30	31	1
2	3	4	5	6	7	8
9	10	11	12	13	14	15
16	17	18	19	20	21	22
23	24	25	26	27	28	29
30						

DECEMBER

S	M	T	W	TH	F	S
30	1	2	3	4	5	6
7	8	9	10	11	12	13
14	15	16	17	18	19	20
21	22	23	24	25	26	27
28	29	30	31	1	2	3

2026

JANUARY

S	M	T	W	TH	F	S
28	29	30	31	1	2	3
4	5	6	7	8	9	10
11	12	13	14	15	16	17
18	19	20	21	22	23	24
25	26	27	28	29	30	31

FEBRUARY

S	M	T	W	TH	F	S
1	2	3	4	5	6	7
8	9	10	11	12	13	14
15	16	17	18	19	20	21
22	23	24	25	26	27	28
1	2	3	4	5	6	7

MARCH

S	M	T	W	TH	F	S
1	2	3	4	5	6	7
8	9	10	11	12	13	14
15	16	17	18	19	20	21
22	23	24	25	26	27	28
29	30	31	1	2	3	4

APRIL

S	M	T	W	TH	F	S
29	30	31	1	2	3	4
5	6	7	8	9	10	11
12	13	14	15	16	17	18
19	20	21	22	23	24	25
26	27	28	29	30	1	2

MAY

S	M	T	W	TH	F	S
26	27	28	29	30	1	2
3	4	5	6	7	8	9
10	11	12	13	14	15	16
17	18	19	20	21	22	23
24	25	26	27	28	29	30
31						

JUNE

S	M	T	W	TH	F	S
31	1	2	3	4	5	6
7	8	9	10	11	12	13
14	15	16	17	18	19	20
21	22	23	24	25	26	27
28	29	30	1	2	3	4

JULY

S	M	T	W	TH	F	S
28	29	30	1	2	3	4
5	6	7	8	9	10	11
12	13	14	15	16	17	18
19	20	21	22	23	24	25
26	27	28	29	30	31	1

AUGUST

S	M	T	W	TH	F	S
26	27	28	29	30	31	1
2	3	4	5	6	7	8
9	10	11	12	13	14	15
16	17	18	19	20	21	22
23	24	25	26	27	28	29
30	31					

SEPTEMBER

S	M	T	W	TH	F	S
30	31	1	2	3	4	5
6	7	8	9	10	11	12
13	14	15	16	17	18	19
20	21	22	23	24	25	26
27	28	29	30	1	2	3

OCTOBER

S	M	T	W	TH	F	S
27	28	29	30	1	2	3
4	5	6	7	8	9	10
11	12	13	14	15	16	17
18	19	20	21	22	23	24
25	26	27	28	29	30	31

NOVEMBER

S	M	T	W	TH	F	S
1	2	3	4	5	6	7
8	9	10	11	12	13	14
15	16	17	18	19	20	21
22	23	24	25	26	27	28
29	30	1	2	3	4	5

DECEMBER

S	M	T	W	TH	F	S
29	30	1	2	3	4	5
6	7	8	9	10	11	12
13	14	15	16	17	18	19
20	21	22	23	24	25	26
27	28	29	30	31	1	2

SUNDAY DECEMBER 29

DECEMBER 31, 1977 Kenyan writer Ngũgĩ wa Thiong'o is imprisoned for cowriting a play critical of the Kenyan government.

> "We the workers in factories and plantations said in one voice:
> We reject slave wages!
> Do you remember the 1948 general strike?"
>
> —NGŨGĨ WA THIONG'O AND NGŨGĨ WA MIRII, *I WILL MARRY WHEN I WANT*

JANUARY 1, 1994 Zapatista forces overtake towns in Chiapas, beginning an ongoing revolution against the Mexican state. "The dispossessed, we are millions, and we thereby call upon our brothers and sisters to join this struggle as the only path."

—ZAPATISTA ARMY OF NATIONAL LIBERATION

MONDAY DECEMBER 30

JANUARY 1, 2009 Oscar Grant III was a twenty-two-year-old black man, fatally shot by an Oakland, California, transit cop in the early morning hours of the New Year. The riots that followed were some of the largest the United States had seen in decades. "Oscar Grant: Murdered. The Whole Damn System Is Guilty!"

—PLACARD FROM THE OSCAR GRANT REBELLION

JANUARY 3, 1961 Angolan peasants employed by the Portuguese-Belgium cotton plantation company Cotonang begin protests over poor working conditions, setting off the Angolan struggle for independence from Portugal.

TUESDAY DECEMBER 31

> "Tomorrow we will sing songs of freedom when we commemorate
> the day this slavery ends."
>
> —FIRST PRESIDENT OF ANGOLA AND LEADER OF THE MOVEMENT FOR THE LIBERATION OF ANGOLA ANTÓNIO AGOSTINHO NETO, "FAREWELL AT THE HOUR OF PARTING"

WEDNESDAY JANUARY 1

Subcomandante Marcos and Comandante Tacho in La Realidad, Chiapas, 1999

THURSDAY JANUARY 2

NOTES:

FRIDAY JANUARY 3

SATURDAY JANUARY 4

SUNDAY JANUARY 5

JANUARY 5, 1971 Angela Davis—black feminist, philosopher, and prison abolitionist—declares her innocence in a California court over the kidnapping and murder of a judge. "Prisons do not disappear problems, they disappear human beings. And the practice of disappearing vast numbers of people from poor, immigrant, and racially marginalized communities has literally become big business." —"MASKED RACISM"

JANUARY 6, 1977 Charter 77, a document criticizing the Czech government for its human rights record, is published; it is violently suppressed.

MONDAY JANUARY 6

JANUARY 7, 1957 Djamila Bouhired, the "Arab Joan of Arc" and member of the National Liberation Front, sets off a bomb in an Algiers café, precipitating the Battle of Algiers, a pivotal episode in the Algerian struggle for independence against the French. "It was the most beautiful day of my life because I was confident that I was going to be dying for the sake of the most wonderful story in the world."

JANUARY 9, 1959 Rigoberta Menchú Tum, indigenous revolutionary and Nobel Peace Prize winner, is born in Chimel, Guatemala. "[My cause] wasn't born out of something good, it was born out of wretchedness and bitterness. It has been radicalized by the poverty in which my people live." —I, RIGOBERTA MENCHÚ

TUESDAY JANUARY 7

JANUARY 11, 1894 Donghak Rebellion begins in Mujiang, Korea, over local corruption, eventually growing into an anti-establishment movement. "The people are the root of the nation. If the root withers, the nation will be enfeebled." —DONGHAK REBELLION PROCLAMATION

WEDNESDAY JANUARY 8

Rigoberta Menchú Tum, indigenous revolutionary and Nobel Peace Prize winner

THURSDAY JANUARY 9

NOTES:

FRIDAY JANUARY 10

SATURDAY JANUARY 11

SUNDAY JANUARY 12

MONDAY JANUARY 13

TUESDAY JANUARY 14

JANUARY 12, 1904 Herero soldiers rebel against German colonial rule in present-day Namibia. It is estimated that the Herero population was reduced from 80,000 to 15,000 in the following three years through systematic violence and deportation.

JANUARY 13, 1898 Émile Zola publishes his infamous letter, "J'accuse...!," accusing the French government of framing Jewish general Alfred Dreyfus for sabotage.

JANUARY 15, 1919 Rosa Luxemburg, founder of the Spartacus League, is murdered by the German Social Democratic government. "The madness will cease and the bloody demons of hell will vanish only when workers in Germany and France, England and Russia finally awake from their stupor, extend to each other a brotherly hand, and drown out the bestial chorus of imperialist war-mongers." —*JUNIUS PAMPHLET*

JANUARY 17, 1893 Queen Lili'uokalani, Hawaii's last monarch, is overthrown by American colonists.

JANUARY 17, 1961 Patrice Lumumba, Congolese independence leader and first prime minister of independent Congo, is assassinated by the Belgian government. Six months earlier, he had been deposed in a CIA-backed coup. "They are trying to distort your focus when they call our government a communist government, in the pay of the Soviet Union, or say that Lumumba is a communist, an anti-white: Lumumba is an African."

WEDNESDAY JANUARY 15

Patrice Lumumba (1925–1961) raises his unshackled arms
following his release, 1960

THURSDAY JANUARY 16

NOTES:

FRIDAY JANUARY 17

SATURDAY JANUARY 18

SUNDAY JANUARY 19

MONDAY JANUARY 20

TUESDAY JANUARY 21

JANUARY 20, 1973 Amílcar Cabral, a communist intellectual and guerrilla leader of Guinea-Bissau's anti-colonial movement against the Portuguese, is assassinated. Guinea-Bissau became independent just months later.

JANUARY 20, 2017 Hundreds of protesters are arrested in Washington, DC, as Donald Trump is inaugurated as US president. The following day, an estimated 470,000 people rally for the Women's March on Washington. "Pussy Grabs Back." —PROTEST SLOGAN

JANUARY 21, 1935 The Wilderness Society is founded by conservationists; it would become one of the most radical US environmentalist groups into the 1970s. "Our bigger-and-better society is now like a hypochondriac, so obsessed with its own economic health as to have lost the capacity to remain healthy." —SOCIETY FOUNDER ALDO LEOPOLD, *A SAND COUNTY ALMANAC*

JANUARY 22, 1936 Burmese student union leaders Aung San and U Nu are expelled for criticizing British rule in Burma, leading to a national student strike. "Escaped from Awizi a devil in the form of a black dog ... Will finder please kick him back to hell." —NYO MYA, "HELL HOUND AT LARGE"

JANUARY 23, 1976 Paul Robeson, the African American singer and civil rights campaigner, dies. "I stand always on the side of those who will toil and labor. As an artist I come to sing, but as a citizen, I will always speak for peace, and no one can silence me in this."

JANUARY 24, 1911 The anarcho-feminist Kanno Sugako is hanged for plotting to assassinate Emperor Meiji. "In accordance with long-standing customs, we have been seen as a form of material property. Women in Japan are in a state of slavery." —"WOMEN ARE SLAVES"

WEDNESDAY JANUARY 22

Activist, singer, and actor Paul Robeson (1898–1976)

THURSDAY JANUARY 23

NOTES:

FRIDAY JANUARY 24

SATURDAY JANUARY 25

V

TEN MYTHS ABOUT ISRAEL
ILAN PAPPE

Colonialism can be described as the movement of Europeans to different parts of the world, creating new "white" nations where indigenous people had once had their own kingdoms. These nations could only be created if the settlers employed two logics: the logic of elimination—getting rid by all means possible of the indigenous people, including by genocide; and the logic of dehumanization—regarding the non-Europeans as inferior and thus as not deserving the same rights as the settlers. In South Africa these twin logics led to the creation of the apartheid system, founded officially in 1948, the same year that the Zionist movement translated the same logics into an ethnic cleansing operation in Palestine.

From a settler colonial perspective events such as the occupation of the West Bank and the Gaza Strip, the Oslo Process, and the disengagement from Gaza in 2005 are all part of the same Israeli strategy of taking as much of Palestine as possible with as few Palestinians in it as possible. The means of achieving this

goal have changed over time, and it remains uncompleted. However, it is the main fuel that feeds the fire of the conflict.

The exceptionalism enjoyed by Israel, and before that by the Zionist movement, makes a mockery of any Western critique of human rights abuses in the Arab world. Any discussion of the abuse of the Palestinians' human rights needs to include an understanding of the inevitable outcome of settler colonial projects such as Zionism. The Jewish settlers are now an organic and integral part of the land. They cannot, and will not, be removed. They should be part of the future, but not on the basis of the constant oppression and dispossession of the local Palestinians.

There are deep layers of history that will need to be addressed if a genuine attempt is to be made at a resolution. After World War II, Zionism was allowed to become a colonialist project at a time when colonialism was being rejected by the civilized world because the creation of a Jewish state offered Europe,

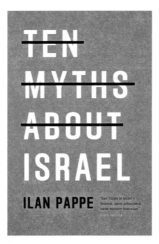

TEN MYTHS ABOUT ISRAEL

ILAN PAPPE

"Ilan Pappe is Israel's bravest, most principled, most incisive historian"
JOHN PILGER

and West Germany in particular, an easy way out of the worst excesses of anti-Semitism ever seen. Israel was the first to declare its recognition of "a new Germany"—in return it received a lot of money, but also, far more importantly, a carte blanche to turn the whole of Palestine into Israel. Zionism offered itself as the solution to anti-Semitism but became the main reason for its continued presence. The "deal" also failed to uproot the racism and xenophobia that still lies at the heart of Europe, and which produced Nazism on the continent and a brutal colonialism outside of it. That racism and xenophobia is now turned against Muslims and Islam; since it is intimately connected to the Israel–Palestinian question, it could be reduced once a genuine answer to that question is found.

We all deserve a better ending to the story of the Holocaust. This could involve a strong multicultural Germany showing the way to the rest of Europe; an American society dealing bravely with the racial crimes of its past

that still resonate today; an Arab world that expunges its barbarism and inhumanity ... Nothing like that could happen if we continue to fall into the trap of treating mythologies as truths. Palestine was not empty and the Jewish people had homelands; Palestine was colonized, not "redeemed"; and its people were dispossessed in 1948, rather than leaving voluntarily.

Colonized people, even under the UN Charter, have the right to struggle for their liberation, even with an army, and the successful ending to such a struggle lies in the creation of a democratic state that includes all of its inhabitants. A discussion of the future, liberated from the ten myths about Israel, will hopefully not only help to bring peace to Israel and Palestine, but will also help Europe reach a proper closure on the horrors of World War II and the dark era of colonialism.

This is an edited excerpt from Ten Myths about Israel *by Ilan Pappe (Verso Books, 2024).*

SUNDAY JANUARY 26

JANUARY 27, 1924 Lenin's funeral takes place in Red Square. In attendance was the poet Vladimir Mayakovsky, who went on to pen the epic poem "Vladimir Ilyich Lenin."

"Just guzzling
        snoozing
                and pocketing pelf,
Capitalism
        got lazy and feeble."

JANUARY 28, 1948 A plane crash kills twenty-eight bracero farm workers being sent back to Mexico. Cesar Chavez considered the moment part of his early political education.

MONDAY JANUARY 27

JANUARY 29, 1967 Arusha Declaration, written by Julius Nyerere, is issued to clarify Tanzania's path toward Ujamaa, or African socialism. "We, in Africa, have no more need of being 'converted' to socialism than we have of being 'taught' democracy."
—"UJAMAA, THE BASIS OF AFRICAN SOCIALISM"

JANUARY 30, 1972 British soldiers shot twenty-eight unarmed civilians in Northern Ireland during a peaceful protest march against internment, in what become known as Bloody Sunday—one of the most significant brutal events of the Troubles.

FEBRUARY 1, 1902 Langston Hughes, poet and figure of the Harlem Renaissance, is born.

TUESDAY JANUARY 28

"What happens to a dream deferred?
Does it dry up
like a raisin in the sun?
Or fester like a sore—
and then run?"
        —"MONTAGE OF A DREAM DEFERRED"

WEDNESDAY JANUARY 29

The 35th Bloody Sunday memorial march in Derry, January 28, 2007

THURSDAY JANUARY 30

NOTES:

FRIDAY JANUARY 31

SATURDAY FEBRUARY 1

SUNDAY FEBRUARY 2

FEBRUARY 2, 1512 Taíno hero Hatuey is captured and killed after besieging the Spaniards for four months at their first fort in Cuba. "[Gold] is the God the Spaniards worship. For these they fight and kill, for these they persecute us and that is why we have to throw them into the sea." —HATUEY'S SPEECH TO THE TAÍNOS

FEBRUARY 3, 1930 The Indochinese Communist Party is established; it conducted an underground struggle against the French colonialists and, later, the American invaders.

FEBRUARY 4, 1899 Philippine-American War begins after the Philippine government objects to being handed over to the US from Spain.

MONDAY FEBRUARY 3

"The North
Americans have
captured nothing
but a vessel
of water,
nothing that
our sun
will find difficult
to empty with its rage."

—ALFREDO NAVARRO SALANGA

TUESDAY FEBRUARY 4

FEBRUARY 7, 1948 Tens of thousands of silent marchers in Bogotá memorialize victims of Colombian state violence. "Señor Presidente, our flag is in mourning; this silent multitude, the mute cry from our hearts, asks only that you treat us ... as you would have us treat you." —JORGE ELIÉCER GAITÁN, LEADER OF THE COLOMBIAN LIBERAL PARTY

FEBRUARY 8, 1996 John Perry Barlow publishes "A Declaration of the Independence of Cyberspace" in response to an anti-pornography bill passed by the US Congress that would have chilled online speech dramatically. "On behalf of the future, I ask you of the past to leave us alone."

WEDNESDAY FEBRUARY 5

Torture of Hatuey in Cuba, by Theodor de Bry, 1590

THURSDAY FEBRUARY 6

NOTES:

FRIDAY FEBRUARY 7

SATURDAY FEBRUARY 8

SUNDAY FEBRUARY 9

MONDAY FEBRUARY 10

TUESDAY FEBRUARY 11

FEBRUARY 10, 1883 The Russian revolutionary Vera Figner is arrested for her role in Tsar Alexander II's assassination. She received a death sentence that was later commuted. "My past experience had convinced me that the only way to change the existing order was by force." —*MEMOIRS OF A REVOLUTIONIST*

FEBRUARY 11, 1916 Emma Goldman, anarchist agitator, publisher and all-around "rebel woman," is arrested for distributing a pamphlet about birth control written by Margaret Sanger.

FEBRUARY 11, 1990 Nelson Mandela is freed after twenty-seven years as a political prisoner. Four years later he became the first president of post-apartheid South Africa.

FEBRUARY 13, 1967 Forough Farrokhzad, feminist poet who has inspired much debate in Iran about modernity, dies in a car crash. "If you want these bonds broken, grasp the skirt of obstinacy." —"CALL TO ARMS"

FEBRUARY 14, 1818 The birth date chosen by Frederick Douglass, America's foremost abolitionist writer and activist. "What, to the American slave, is your 4th of July? I answer: a day that reveals to him, more than all other days in the year, the gross injustice and cruelty to which he is the constant victim." —"THE MEANING OF JULY FOURTH FOR THE NEGRO"

FEBRUARY 15, 1855 Mukta Salve, a fourteen-year-old Dalit, publishes the earliest surviving piece of writing by an "untouchable" woman. "Let that religion, where only one person is privileged and the rest are deprived, perish from the earth and let it never enter our minds to be proud of such a religion." —"ABOUT THE GRIEFS OF THE MANGS AND MAHARS"

WEDNESDAY FEBRUARY 12

Nelson Rolihlahla Mandela (1918–2013), anti-apartheid activist and first president of South Africa

THURSDAY FEBRUARY 13

NOTES:

FRIDAY FEBRUARY 14

SATURDAY FEBRUARY 15

SUNDAY FEBRUARY 16

MONDAY FEBRUARY 17

TUESDAY FEBRUARY 18

FEBRUARY 17, 1958 The Campaign for Nuclear Disarmament is founded in Britain; it would become the country's most important protest movement during the late 1950s and early 1960s. "Sanity is always hardest to restore at the summit—the air here is rarified. It seems to affect the brain. We can assert it at the base." —ACTIVIST ALEX COMFORT'S SPEECH AT THE INAUGURAL MEETING

FEBRUARY 18, 1934 Black lesbian poet Audre Lorde is born in New York City.

"For all of us
this instant and this triumph
We were never meant to survive."
  —"A LITANY FOR SURVIVAL"

FEBRUARY 19, 1942 Japanese American internment begins in the US through Executive Order 9066.

FEBRUARY 19, 1963 Betty Friedan's *The Feminine Mystique*, a classic of second-wave feminism, is published. "The problem lay buried, unspoken, for many years in the minds of American women."

FEBRUARY 21, 1848 The *Communist Manifesto*, written by Friedrich Engels and Karl Marx, is published. "The proletarians have nothing to lose but their chains. They have a world to win."

FEBRUARY 21, 1965 Malcolm X is assassinated at the Audubon Ballroom in New York City. "Uncle Sam's hands are dripping with blood, dripping with the blood of the black man in this country." —"THE BALLOT OR THE BULLET"

WEDNESDAY FEBRUARY 19

Audre Lorde (1943–1992)

THURSDAY FEBRUARY 20

NOTES:

FRIDAY FEBRUARY 21

SATURDAY FEBRUARY 22

THE POWER OF UNIONS
JEFF SCHUHRKE

There is power in a union. Not only the power to secure pay raises and employee benefits, but also—as the 1963 general strike in British Guiana demonstrates—the power to bring economies to a halt and overthrow governments. In the latter half of the twentieth century, the American foreign policy establishment wholly recognized this power. US officials particularly understood that labor movements abroad would play a decisive role in determining the outcome of the Cold War contest for worldwide ideological, geopolitical, and economic supremacy. Coming out of the crises of the Great Depression and World War II, and fearing the growing influence of communism, Washington planners built what was intended to be a well-managed international capitalist system backed by US economic and military power. This system would be protected and expanded through what many scholars call an "informal empire," based not on outright territorial conquest but on political, economic, and cultural dominance. In administering such an informal empire, where indirect influence rather than explicit control was often (though hardly always) the modus operandi, the American state would exert power through numerous nongovernment subsidiaries. These included financial institutions, business associations, scholarly societies, news outlets, publishing houses, political parties, private charities, student organizations—and, importantly, trade unions.

*

The world we inhabit today—one in which capital flows effortlessly across nations and multibillionaires take joyrides into outer space while a subjugated global working class remains bounded by militarized borders on an ecologically degraded planet—was shaped most decisively by the US government's actions during the Cold War. The American labor movement was perhaps the only organized force that could have exerted the necessary outside pressure to alter Washington's calculus, and thus alter the fate of the world. Instead, AFL-CIO officials, without consulting the millions of workers they represented, chose to be partners in the making of an unequal international order dominated by capital. Understanding why and how this happened is essential for all those who want to build the kind of multiracial, inclusive, international working-class movement that is necessary in the twenty-first century to overcome oppression, militarism, and exploitation around the world. Reckoning with this history is therefore the responsibility of every serious trade unionist and labor advocate in the United States.

*

Organized labor around the world should be striving toward the creation of a truly unified working-class movement, dependent on its own collective strength and dedicated to replacing capitalism with socialism and militarism with peace. While this may seem obvious, it historically has not been the official approach of the AFL-CIO and its affiliated unions, which, at their worst, have assisted the US government around the world in dividing workers, suppressing democracy, waging unjust wars, and foiling progressive movements. Hope for global labor unity ultimately lies in the ability of trade unionists everywhere to put class solidarity above national allegiance, and to act with their fellow workers, whoever and wherever they may be, for their collective liberation and mutual survival. With the US working class now more "international" than it has ever been—composed of people of a multitude of nationalities, ethnicities, races, religions, languages, and cultures—identifying exactly how to achieve and maintain this kind of class unity, and translate it into effective action, can perhaps begin at home. If they are to be serious vehicles for strengthening and protecting the working class both at home and abroad in this era of overlapping crises, today's AFL-CIO and its affiliated unions must adopt the kind of principled labor internationalism that would inevitably bring them into conflict

with US foreign policy instead of reflexively serving it. But a labor movement that places class struggle and anti-imperialism ahead of deference to Washington's international designs will not come into being unless workers, both within and outside the AFL-CIO, build it themselves.

This is an edited excerpt from Blue-Collar Empire: The Untold Story of US Labor's Global Anticommunist Crusade by Jeff Schuhrke (Verso Books, 2024).

SUNDAY FEBRUARY 23

MONDAY FEBRUARY 24

TUESDAY FEBRUARY 25

FEBRUARY 23, 1934 George Padmore, leading Pan-Africanist born in Trinidad, is expelled from the Comintern and shifts his focus to African independence struggles: "The black man certainly has to pay dear for carrying the white man's burden."

FEBRUARY 24, 1895 Cuba's final War of Independence from Spain begins, planned in part by poet and revolutionary philosopher José Martí. "A cloud of ideas is a thing no armored prow can smash through." —"OUR AMERICA"

FEBRUARY 26, 1906 Upton Sinclair's exposé on the meat packing industry, *The Jungle*, is published, prompting the enactment of the Meat Inspection and Pure Food and Drug Acts.

FEBRUARY 27, 1973 Oglala Lakota and American Indian Movement members, including Leonard Peltier, begin an occupation of Wounded Knee, South Dakota, on the Pine Ridge Indian Reservation.

MARCH 1, 1896 Ethiopian fighters defeat Italian forces at the Battle of Adwa, securing Ethiopian sovereignty to become a symbol of African resistance against European colonialism. "Once a white snake has bitten you, you will find no cure for it." —ETHIOPIAN REBEL LEADER BAHTA HAGOS

MARCH 1, 1940 Richard Wright's seminal novel *Native Son*, about a black youth living on Chicago's South Side, is published. His writings would shift the US discourse on race.

MARCH 1, 1954 Lolita Lebrón and comrades open fire on the US House of Representatives in the struggle for Puerto Rican independence. "I did not come to kill anyone, I came to die for Puerto Rico." —LEBRÓN, WORDS UPON ARREST

WEDNESDAY FEBRUARY 26

Lolita Lebrón (1919–2010) following her arrest in 1954

THURSDAY FEBRUARY 27

NOTES:

FRIDAY FEBRUARY 28

SATURDAY MARCH 1

SUNDAY MARCH 2

MONDAY MARCH 3

TUESDAY MARCH 4

MARCH 2, 1444 Albanian resistance leader Skanderbeg founds the League of Lezhë, uniting Balkan chieftains to fight the invading Ottoman army.

MARCH 6, 1923 The Egyptian Feminist Union is established. "They rise in times of trouble when the wills of men are tried." —ACTIVIST HUDA SHAARAWI, *HAREM YEARS: THE MEMOIRS OF AN EGYPTIAN FEMINIST, 1879–1924*

MARCH 6, 1957 The leader of the Gold Coast's anti-imperialist fight against the British, Pan-Africanist Kwame Nkrumah, becomes the first prime minister of independent Ghana.

MARCH 6, 1984 Coal miners walk out at Cortonwood Colliery in South Yorkshire, beginning the yearlong UK miner's strike, the longest in history. "I'd rather be a picket than a scab." —PICKET LINE SLOGAN

MARCH 7, 1921 At the Kronstadt naval base, Russia's Red Army attacks sailors, soldiers, and civilians who are protesting widespread famine and the Bolshevik repression of strikes.

MARCH 7, 1942 Lucy Parsons, anarchist and Industrial Workers of the World cofounder who was born in slavery, dies in Chicago. "Stroll you down the avenues of the rich and look through the magnificent plate windows into their voluptuous homes, and here you will discover the *very identical robbers* who have despoiled you and yours." —"TO TRAMPS"

MARCH 8, 1914 First International Women's Day, cofounded by German Marxist Clara Zetkin, is established on this day of the year. "What made women's labour particularly attractive to the capitalists was not only its lower price but also the greater submissiveness of women."

WEDNESDAY MARCH 5

Lucy Parsons (1853–1942) after her arrest for rioting at a 1915 unemployment protest

THURSDAY MARCH 6

NOTES:

FRIDAY MARCH 7

SATURDAY MARCH 8

SUNDAY MARCH 9

MONDAY MARCH 10

TUESDAY MARCH 11

MARCH 9, 1951 Pakistani intellectuals and military officials are arrested in the Rawalpindi Conspiracy plan to overthrow the anticommunist government.

MARCH 12, 1930 Mohandas Gandhi begins the Salt Satyagraha, challenging the British Raj. "I know the dangers attendant upon the methods adopted by me. But the country is not likely to mistake my meaning."

MARCH 13, 1933 The poet Abdukhaliq Uyghur is executed by the Chinese government for encouraging rebellion and supporting Uyghur independence.

MARCH 13, 1979 Maurice Bishop's New Jewel Movement overthrows the Grenada government, the first armed socialist revolution in a predominantly black country outside of Africa.

MARCH 14, 2008 Riots break out in Lhasa and spread throughout Tibet, targeting Han Chinese residents and businesses. "The oppressors' snipers are still standing above Tibetan people's heads; on sunny days, the beams deflected from the guns in their hands stab into the prostrating Tibetans. This is a collective memory which has been engraved on Tibetan people's hearts." —TIBETAN POET WOESER

MARCH 15, 1845 Friedrich Engels publishes *The Condition of the Working Class in England*.

MARCH 15, 1960 A student demonstration against the fraudulent election victory of South Korean strongman Syngman Rhee was attacked by police. One month later, the body of student protester Kim Ju-yul washed ashore, his skull split open by a tear-gas grenade. The public outrage would eventually result in the April Revolution, which would end Rhee's rule.

WEDNESDAY MARCH 12

Abdukhaliq Uyghur (1901–1933), Uyghur poet

THURSDAY MARCH 13

NOTES:

FRIDAY MARCH 14

SATURDAY MARCH 15

SUNDAY MARCH 16

MONDAY MARCH 17

TUESDAY MARCH 18

MARCH 18, 1834 Six farm workers from Tolpuddle, England, are sentenced to penal transportation to Australia for forming a trade union. "Labour is the poor man's property, from which all protection is withheld. Has not then the working man as much right to preserve and protect his labour as the rich man has his capital?" —TOLPUDDLE MARTYR GEORGE LOVELESS, *THE VICTIMS OF WHIGGERY*

MARCH 18, 1871 Paris Commune is established, a participatory workers' democracy. "Workers, make no mistake—this is an all-out war, a war between parasites and workers, exploiters and producers." —COMMUNARDS, "DECLARATION BY THE CENTRAL COMMITTEE OF THE NATIONAL GUARD"

MARCH 19, 2005 First road blockade in Kennedy Road settlement in Durban, South Africa, that would become the Abahlali baseMjondolo ("shack dwellers") movement.

MARCH 21, 1960 South African police kill sixty-nine protesters in the Sharpeville Massacre, forcing the anti-apartheid movement underground.

MARCH 23, 1775 Patrick Henry, who became the first post-colonial governor of Virginia, delivers his "Give Me Liberty" speech. "There is no retreat, but in submission and slavery! Our chains are forged! Their clanking may be heard on the plains of Boston! The war is inevitable—and let it come!"

MARCH 23, 1918 Avant-garde artist Tristan Tzara issues the Dada Manifesto, a politico-artistic movement whose anti-bourgeois stance would influence the Situationists and the Beats. "DADA DADA DADA—the roar of contorted pains, the interweaving of contraries and all contradictions, freaks and irrelevancies: LIFE."

WEDNESDAY MARCH 19

Paris Commune: a barricade on Rue Voltaire, after its capture by
the regular army during the Bloody Week, May 1871

THURSDAY MARCH 20

NOTES:

FRIDAY MARCH 21

SATURDAY MARCH 22

SUNDAY MARCH 23

MARCH 23, 1931 Revolutionary Bhagat Singh, who threw a bomb into India's central legislative assembly, is hanged by the British Raj. "Let me tell you, British rule is here not because God wills it but because they possess power and we do not dare to oppose them." —"WHY I AM AN ATHEIST"

MARCH 24, 1977 Argentine journalist Rodolfo Walsh publishes his "Open Letter from a Writer to the Military Junta," accusing them of disappearing thousands of Argentines. The next day he is murdered. "They are the victims of a doctrine of collective guilt, which long ago disappeared from the norms of justice of any civilized community."

MONDAY MARCH 24

MARCH 24, 1980 Oscar Romero, archbishop of San Salvador in El Salvador and critic of the Salvadorean death squads, is assassinated while giving mass. "We are your people. The peasants you kill are your own brothers and sisters."

MARCH 24, 1987 First demonstration of ACT UP, pioneering direct-action AIDS organization, on Wall Street to protest Food and Drug Administration inaction on drug development. "Silence = Death" —ACT UP LOGO

MARCH 27, 1969 First national Chicano Youth Conference is hosted in Denver by Crusade for Justice, the civil rights organization founded by former boxer Corky Gonzáles.

TUESDAY MARCH 25

MARCH 29, 1942 The Hukbalahap (Philippine communist guerrilla organization) is founded; its insurgency against the government lasts eight years. "Our friends in Manila refer to us as being 'outside.' That is incorrect terminology ... We are on the inside of the struggle." —PEASANT LEADER LUIS TARUC, *BORN OF THE PEOPLE*

WEDNESDAY MARCH 26

Rodolfo "Corky" Gonzáles (1928–2005), Mexican American boxer, poet, and political activist

THURSDAY MARCH 27

NOTES:

FRIDAY MARCH 28

SATURDAY MARCH 29

SUNDAY MARCH 30

MONDAY MARCH 31

TUESDAY APRIL 1

APRIL 1, 1649 Poor farmers begin digging plots at Saint George's Hill in Surrey, in one of the first acts of the Digger movement that sought to abolish property and wages, in some instances by occupying common land. "We are resolved to be cheated no longer, nor be held under the slavish fear of you no longer, seeing the Earth was made for us, as well as for you." —MOVEMENT FOUNDER GERRARD WINSTANLEY, "DECLARATION FROM THE POOR OPPRESSED PEOPLE OF ENGLAND"

APRIL 3, 1874 Wong Chin Foo, publisher of the first Chinese American newspaper, is naturalized as a US citizen. "The difference between the heathen and the Christian is that the heathen does good for the sake of doing good."

APRIL 3, 1895 Playwright and essayist Oscar Wilde goes on trial for homosexual activity and is imprisoned for two years. "It is immoral to use private property in order to alleviate the horrible evils that result from the institution of private property." —"THE SOUL OF MAN UNDER SOCIALISM"

APRIL 4, 1968 Martin Luther King Jr. is assassinated. "A true revolution of values will soon look uneasily on the glaring contrast of poverty and wealth." —"BEYOND VIETNAM: A TIME TO BREAK SILENCE"

APRIL 5, 1971 The "Manifesto of the 343," signed by 343 women (including Simone de Beauvoir) who had had secret abortions, demands that the French government legalize the procedure.

APRIL 5, 1976 On the traditional day of mourning, thousands of Beijingers lay wreaths and poems on Tiananmen Square, indirectly criticizing the Cultural Revolution.

"If a thousand challengers lie beneath your feet, Count me as number thousand and one." —BEI DAO, "THE ANSWER," WHICH BECAME AN ANTHEM OF THE DEMOCRACY MOVEMENT

WEDNESDAY APRIL 2

Dr. Martin Luther King Jr. (1929–1968) being arrested in 1956 during the Montgomery Bus Boycott

THURSDAY APRIL 3

NOTES:

FRIDAY APRIL 4

SATURDAY APRIL 5

SUNDAY APRIL 6

MONDAY APRIL 7

TUESDAY APRIL 8

APRIL 8, 1950 Imprisoned for sedition, the revolutionary Turkish poet Nâzim Hikmet launches a hunger strike for amnesty for political prisoners.

"Galloping from farthest Asia
and jutting into the Mediterranean
like a mare's head
this country is ours."
—"INVITATION"

APRIL 9, 1553 François Rabelais dies; he is the author of *Gargantua and Pantagruel*, an early novel that subverted the Renaissance social order.

APRIL 10, 1919 Emiliano Zapata, Mexican Revolution leader, is assassinated by the government. "The nation is tired of false men and traitors who make promises like liberators and who on arriving in power forget them and constitute themselves as tyrants."

APRIL 11, 1981 Riots break out in the Caribbean London neighborhood of Brixton in response to police targeting of young black men under the sus law. The fighting lasts for three days.

APRIL 11, 2007 Kurt Vonnegut, author of novels with anti-authoritarian and anti-war themes, dies.

WEDNESDAY APRIL 9

The Brixton Riots, 1981

THURSDAY APRIL 10

NOTES:

FRIDAY APRIL 11

SATURDAY APRIL 12

SUNDAY APRIL 13

MONDAY APRIL 14

TUESDAY APRIL 15

APRIL 13, 1635 Fakhr al-Din II, Druze independence leader against the Ottoman Empire and Lebanon's first freedom fighter, is executed. "No promise of reward or threat of punishment will dissuade us." —MESSAGE TO THE PEOPLE

APRIL 14, 1428 Vietnamese forces are victorious after a ten-year rebellion against their Chinese rulers. "Today it is a case of the grasshopper pitted against the elephant. But tomorrow the elephant will have its guts ripped out." —REBELLION LEADER LÊ LỢI'S VICTORY SPEECH

APRIL 14, 2002 Venezuelan president Hugo Chávez, who described his socialist movement as the Bolivarian Revolution, returns to power after having been ousted in a US-backed coup two days earlier. "What we now have to do is define the future of the world. Dawn is breaking out all over." —ADDRESS TO THE UN GENERAL ASSEMBLY

APRIL 15, 1936 The Great Revolt begins in Palestine against British Mandate and Zionism, lasting three years. "They stepped all over us until we couldn't take any more. This went on until the rebellion was smashed." —MAHMOUD ABOU DEEB, WITNESS TO THE REVOLT

APRIL 15, 1960 The civil rights group Student Nonviolent Coordinating Committee is founded in Raleigh, North Carolina. It played a major role in the sit-ins and freedom rides of the 1960s.

APRIL 18, 1955 Twenty-nine newly independent African and Asian countries meet at the Bandung Conference in Indonesia, in a show of strength for the Non-Aligned Movement. "Without peace, our independence means little." —OPENING SPEECH BY INDONESIAN LEADER SUKARNO

WEDNESDAY APRIL 16

Palestinian Arabs meet at Abu Ghosh during the Great Revolt, 1936

THURSDAY APRIL 17

NOTES:

FRIDAY APRIL 18

SATURDAY APRIL 19

SUNDAY APRIL 20

MONDAY APRIL 21

TUESDAY APRIL 22

APRIL 20, 1773 Peter Bestes and others deliver a petition for freedom "in behalf of our fellow slaves" to the Massachusetts legislature. "The divine spirit of freedom seems to fire every human breast on the continent, except such as are bribed to assist in executing the execrable plan."

APRIL 21, 1913 The Indian revolutionary group, the Ghadar Party, is formed by Punjabis in North America.

APRIL 22, 1977 Kenyan activist Wangari Maathai founds the Green Belt Movement, an environmental nonprofit aimed at empowering poor, rural women.

APRIL 23, 1968 Students occupy buildings in New York's Columbia University to protest the school's ties to a defense contractor, triggering a campus-wide strike. "Up against the wall, Motherfuckers!" —PROTEST GRAFFITI

APRIL 24, 1916 Irish republicans mount an armed insurrection against the British imperialists on Easter week, in what became known as the Easter Rising.

APRIL 25, 1974 Portuguese armed forces overthrow the ruling Estado Novo dictatorship in what becomes known as the Carnation Revolution, setting the stage for its colonies to achieve independence.

APRIL 26, 1937 The Basque town of Guernica is destroyed in an aerial bombing by German and Italian forces, in one of the most sordid episodes of the Spanish Civil War.

"Faces good in firelight good in frost
Refusing the night the wounds and blows."
—SURREALIST POET PAUL ELUARD, "VICTORY OF GUERNICA"

WEDNESDAY APRIL 23

UC Berkeley students of the Ghadar Movement, 1915

THURSDAY APRIL 24

NOTES:

FRIDAY APRIL 25

SATURDAY APRIL 26

ISRAEL'S ARCHITECTURE OF OCCUPATION
EYAL WEIZMAN

Against the geography of stable, static places, and the balance across linear and fixed sovereign borders, frontiers are deep, shifting, fragmented and elastic territories. Temporary lines of engagement, marked by makeshift boundaries, are not limited to the edges of political space but exist throughout its depth. Distinctions between the "inside" and "outside" cannot be clearly marked. In fact, the straighter, more geometrical and more abstract official colonial borders across the "New Worlds" tended to be, the more the territories of effective control were fragmented and dynamic and thus unchartable by any conventional mapping technique. The Occupied Palestinian Territories could be seen as such a frontier zone. However, in relation to the dimensions of ancient empires—"optimal," by several accounts, at forty days' horse travel from one end to the other—within the 5,655 square kilometers of the West Bank, the 2.5 million Palestinians and 500,000 Jewish settlers seem to inhabit the head of a pin. In it, as Sharon Rotbard mentioned, "the most explosive ingredients of our time, all modern utopias and all ancient beliefs [are contained] simultaneously and instantaneously, bubbling side by side with no precautions." These territories have become the battlefield on which various agents of state power and independent actors confront each

other, meeting local and international resistance. Within them, the mundane elements of planning and architecture have become tactical tools and the means of dispossession. Under Israel's regime of "erratic occupation," Palestinian life, property and political rights are constantly violated not only by the frequent actions of the Israeli military, but by a process in which their environment is unpredictably and continuously refashioned, tightening around them like a noose.

Accounts of colonialism tend to concentrate on the way systems of governance and control are translated into the organization of space, according to underlying principles of rational organization, classification, procedure and rules of administration. In the Occupied Palestinian Territories, the organization of geographical space cannot simply be understood as the preserve of the Israeli government executive power alone, but rather one diffused among a multiplicity of—often non-state—actors. The spatial organization of the Occupied Territories is a reflection not only of an ordered process of planning and implementation, but, and increasingly so, of "structured chaos," in which the—often deliberate—selective absence of government intervention promotes an unregulated process of violent dispossession. The actors operating within this frontier—young settlers,

HOLLOW LAND

ISRAEL'S ARCHITECTURE OF OCCUPATION

NEW EDITION

EYAL WEIZMAN

the Israeli military, the cellular network provider and other capitalist corporations, human rights and political activists, armed resistance, humanitarian and legal experts, government ministries, foreign governments, "supportive" communities overseas, state planners, the media, the Israeli High Court of Justice—with the differences and contradictions of their aims, all play their part in the diffused and anarchic, albeit collective authorship of its spaces. Because elastic geographies respond to a multiple and diffused rather than a single source of power, their architecture cannot be understood as the material embodiment of a unified political will or as the product of a single ideology. Rather, the organization of the Occupied Territories should be seen as a kind of "political plastic," or as a map of the relation between all the forces that shaped it.

The frontiers of the Occupied Territories are not rigid and fixed; rather, they are elastic, and in constant transformation. The linear border, a cartographic imaginary inherited from the military and political spatiality of the nation state, has splintered into a multitude of temporary, transportable, deployable and removable border-synonyms—"separation walls," "barriers," "blockades," "closures," "road blocks," "checkpoints," "sterile areas," "special security zones," "closed military areas" and "killing zones"—that shrink and expand the territory at will. These borders are dynamic, constantly shifting, ebbing and flowing; they creep along, stealthily surrounding Palestinian villages and roads. They may even erupt into Palestinian living rooms, bursting in through the house walls. The anarchic geography of the frontier is an evolving image of transformation, which is remade and rearranged with every political development or decision. Outposts and settlements might be evacuated and removed, yet new ones are founded and expand. The location of military checkpoints is constantly changing, blocking and modulating Palestinian traffic in ever-differing ways. Mobile military bases create the bridgeheads that maintain the logistics of ever-changing operations. The Israeli military makes incursions into Palestinian towns and refugee camps, occupies them and then withdraws. The Separation Wall, merely one of multiple barriers, is constantly rerouted, its path registering like a seismograph the political and legal battles surrounding it. Where territories appear to be hermetically sealed in by Israeli walls and fences, Palestinian tunnels are dug underneath them. Elastic territories could thus not be understood as benign environments: highly elastic political space is often more dangerous and deadly than a static, rigid one.

This is an edited excerpt from Hollow Land: Israel's Architecture of Occupation *by Eyal Weizman (republished by Verso Books, 2024).*

SUNDAY APRIL 27

APRIL 28, 1967 Heavyweight champion boxer Muhammad Ali refuses induction into the US Armed Forces, leading to a charge for draft evasion and being stripped of his titles. "I ain't got no quarrel with them Vietcong. No Vietcong ever called me nigger."

APRIL 29, 1992 Los Angeles residents begin rioting after the four police officers accused of beating Rodney King are acquitted. "Give us the hammer and the nails, we will rebuild the city." —BLOODS AND CRIPS, "PLAN FOR THE RECONSTRUCTION OF LOS ANGELES"

MAY 1, 1949 Albert Einstein publishes "Why Socialism?" in the inaugural issue of *Monthly Review*. "The economic anarchy of capitalist society as it exists today is, in my opinion, the real source of the evil."

MONDAY APRIL 28

MAY 1, 1970 Lesbian activists deliver their manifesto at the Second Congress to Unite Women in New York City, to protest the exclusion of lesbian speakers. "Lesbian is a label invented by the man to throw at any woman who dares to be his equal." —RADICALESBIANS, "THE WOMAN-IDENTIFIED WOMAN"

MAY 3, 1968 French students protest the closure of the Sorbonne, setting off the May '68 wave of demonstrations and strikes by millions of students and workers. "Be realistic, demand the impossible." —PARIS GRAFFITI

TUESDAY APRIL 29

WEDNESDAY APRIL 30

_____
_____
_____
_____
_____
_____
_____

Boxer and conscientious objector Muhammad Ali in 1966

THURSDAY MAY 1

_____
_____
_____
_____
_____
_____

NOTES:

_____
_____
_____
_____
_____

FRIDAY MAY 2

_____
_____
_____
_____
_____
_____

SATURDAY MAY 3

_____
_____
_____
_____
_____
_____

SUNDAY MAY 4

MAY 4, 1919 Chinese students demonstrate in Beijing, sparking the anti-Confucian New Culture Movement. "Wanting to eat men, at the same time afraid of being eaten themselves, they all eye each other with the deepest suspicion." —LU XUN, "A MADMAN'S DIARY," ONE OF THE MOVEMENT'S REPRESENTATIVE WORKS

MAY 5, 1938 Second and final arrest of Russian poet Osip Mandelstam, for writing critically of Stalin.

"He forges decrees in a line like horseshoes
One for the groin, one the forehead, temple, eye"
—"THE STALIN EPIGRAM"

MONDAY MAY 5

MAY 5, 1966 Jit Phumisak, Thai Marxist poet and revolutionary, is killed after retreating to the jungle with the outlawed Communist Party. "[The Thai people] have been able to identify clearly the enemies who plunder them and skin them alive and suck the very marrow from their bones."
—"THE REAL FACE OF THAI SAKTINA [FEUDALISM] TODAY"

MAY 9, 1918 Scottish revolutionary John Maclean, on trial for sedition for opposing WWI, delivers a rousing speech from the dock. "I am here as the accuser of capitalism, dripping with blood from head to foot."

TUESDAY MAY 6

MAY 11, 1930 Pedro Albizu Campos is elected president of the Puerto Rican Nationalist Party. "The empire is a system. It can wait. It can fatten its victims to render its digestion more enjoyable at a later time."

MAY 10, 1857 Rebellion against British rule in India begins, eventually growing into the First Indian War of Independence.

MAY 10, 1872 Victoria Woodhull, suffragist and publisher of the first English edition of *The Communist Manifesto*, becomes the first woman nominated for president of the US.

WEDNESDAY MAY 7

Victoria Woodhull (1838–1927), suffragist and publisher of the first English edition of *The Communist Manifesto*

THURSDAY MAY 8

NOTES:

FRIDAY MAY 9

SATURDAY MAY 10

SUNDAY MAY 11

MAY 11, 1894 Three thousand employees of the Pullman railcar company go on strike, eventually growing to 250,000 workers before being crushed by federal troops.

MAY 12, 1916 James Connolly is tied to a chair and shot by the British government for his role in the Easter Rising—the precursor to the declaration of the Irish Republic in 1919. Born in Scotland to Irish immigrant parents, Connolly became a leader of the socialist movement in Scotland, Ireland, and the United States, where he was a member of the Socialist Party and the IWW.

MONDAY MAY 12

MAY 13, 1968 French workers join students in a one-day strike, with over a million protesters marching through Paris streets. By the following week, two-thirds of France's workforce was on strike, becoming the largest general strike that had ever stopped the economy of an industrialized country.

MAY 16, 1943 Warsaw Ghetto Uprising, which began in German-occupied Poland to resist the last deportation of Jews to the Treblinka extermination camp, ends in failure. "We decided to gamble for our lives." —MAREK EDELMAN, MEMBER OF THE JEWISH COMBAT ORGANIZATION

TUESDAY MAY 13

MAY 17, 1649 A mutiny in the New Model Army of England by the Levellers, who called for the expansion of suffrage, religious toleration, and sweeping political reforms, is crushed when its leaders are executed. "We do now hold ourselves bound in mutual duty to each other to take the best care we can for the future to avoid both the danger of returning into a slavish condition and the chargeable remedy of another war." —LEVELLERS, "AGREEMENT OF THE PEOPLE"

WEDNESDAY MAY 14

Strikers in Southern France with a sign reading "Factory Occupied by the Workers," 1968

THURSDAY MAY 15

NOTES:

FRIDAY MAY 16

SATURDAY MAY 17

SUNDAY MAY 18

MONDAY MAY 19

TUESDAY MAY 20

MAY 18, 1980 Citizens of Gwangju, South Korea, seize control of their city, demanding democratization, an end to martial law, and an increase in the minimum wage.

MAY 19, 1869 US president Ulysses S. Grant issues the National Eight Hour Law Proclamation, an early but symbolic victory for the struggle over the working day in the US. "Think carefully of the difference between the operative and mechanic leaving his work at half-past seven (after dark, the most of the year), and that of the more leisurely walk home at half-past four p.m., or three hours earlier." —MACHINIST-TURNED-ACTIVIST IRA STEWARD, *THE EIGHT HOUR MOVEMENT*

MAY 19, 1946 Millions of Japanese take part in the Food May Day demonstrations, protesting the country's broken food delivery system.

MAY 21, 1833 William Apess, preacher, politician, and descendant of the Wampanoag King Phillip, joins the Mashpee in Massachusetts in revolt against colonial abuses.

MAY 21, 1998 Suharto resigns as president of Indonesia after three decades of authoritarian rule. "If proposals are rejected without consideration, voices silenced, criticism banned for no reason, accused of subversion and disturbing the peace, then there is only one word: resist!" —"WARNING," WHOSE AUTHOR WIJI THUKUL DISAPPEARED AFTER PARTICIPATING IN ANTI-GOVERNMENT PROTESTS IN 1996

MAY 24, 1798 Society of United Irishmen, a republican group influenced by the American and French revolutions, rises up against English rule in what becomes the Irish Rebellion.

"A wet winter, a dry spring
A bloody summer, and no King."
—IRISH SAYING

WEDNESDAY MAY 21

Demonstrations and riots against Suharto, May 1998

THURSDAY MAY 22

NOTES:

FRIDAY MAY 23

SATURDAY MAY 24

SUNDAY MAY 25

MONDAY MAY 26

TUESDAY MAY 27

MAY 28, 1913 Six hundred black women march through Bloemfontein, South Africa, to protest the law requiring them, as non-white workers, to carry proof of employment.

"Too long have they submitted
to white malignity;
No passes they would carry
but assert their dignity."
—POEM INSPIRED BY THE EVENT, SIGNED "JOHNNY THE OFFICE BOY"

MAY 28, 1918 First Republic of Armenia is declared, following the Armenian Resistance of 1914–18.

MAY 28, 1892 The Sierra Club, which sought to conserve nature and establish national parks, is founded by Scottish-born American John Muir. "Our magnificent redwoods and much of the sugar-pine forests of Sierra Nevada [have] been absorbed by foreign and resident capitalists."—OUR NATIONAL PARKS

MAY 29, 1851 Sojourner Truth, abolitionist speaker, delivers her famous "Ain't I a Woman" speech to the Women's Convention in Akron, Ohio. "I can't read, but I can hear. I have heard the Bible and I learned that Eve caused man to sin. Well, if woman upset the world, do give her a chance to set it right again."

MAY 29, 1963 Peruvian revolutionary Hugo Blanco is captured after leading a "Land or Death" peasant uprising that sparked the country's first agrarian reform. Blanco was spared from execution thanks to pleas from Bertrand Russell, Jean-Paul Sartre, Simone de Beauvoir, Che Guevara, and others. "To be a revolutionary is to love the world, to love life, to be happy."
—"TO MY PEOPLE," WRITTEN FROM EL FRONTÓN PENAL COLONY

WEDNESDAY MAY 28

THURSDAY MAY 29

Armenian Revolutionary Federation fighters, banner reading
"Liberty or Death"

NOTES:

FRIDAY MAY 30

SATURDAY MAY 31

IF ONLY: A NOVEL
VIGDIS HJORTH

She so desperately wanted children in order not to be a child herself but a mother. No longer a daughter but a mother, and the children grounded her, stopped her from floating up into the air or imploding because she didn't know who she was. How can someone who was never whole know where the missing piece lies? She counts the glasses and packs half. She asks him which frying pan he wants. He nods silently in response to all her suggestions. She counts, divides and packs, she carries her desk and chairs from one house to the other through the forest until late at night, she has superhuman strength. Her husband sits in his armchair in front of the television. The children are asleep.

"Do you want this one or that one?" He turns to her.

The tears are streaming down his cheeks, it is the first time in a long time that he has looked at her.

"Not now, Ida," he says. "The king is dead."

The date is in the history books. She got divorced when King Olav died. Young and old walk with tea lights and flowers to the Palace Gardens in the winter darkness, it looks like the scene of a tragedy. She will meet him in May. She is calmer. There is a great deal to keep track of, not to forget. There is the lawyer, the deeds to the house, many bills to pay, but one of her plays will shortly be performed and she is translating another, she reviews, she edits *The Journal*, she will manage. She does it for him. She can't forget him. One day he will come. She writes to him for the first time in a long time. Her writing is calm, she is another person now and in another place. She writes from far away, as if it is the past and she sees it clearly, and somehow it is true: I would have jumped into the deep end with you, she writes.

*

The nights are long and filled with disturbing dreams. What if she will be on her own for ever? The sea is stormy, she is drowning, a boat appears, she waves to it, but it sails on. Even though the man in the boat sees her, he sails on, leaving her to drown. She has a

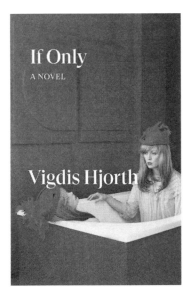

If Only

A NOVEL

Vigdis Hjorth

dream where she lives in a derelict house, it is in ruins. The sink has been smashed as has the lavatory. Yet there are guests whom she must serve, converse with. It means she is letting too many people into her bedroom. She lets in too many people when she really ought to be alone, clearing up and mending. The lavatory is blocked, it overflows with waste. She is bleeding from her arm, from her groin. There are wounds to her body, boils on her face. She is drowning in stinking water and sewage. Her legs sink into the mud, she tries to keep her head above the foul-smelling sewer. She is trying to reach a temple on the shore. A woman walks between the columns, Ida can see her back, she is tall and wearing a Greek tunic with one shoulder bared, then she starts to turn and she may well have a ruined face. All that is missing is that this woman who looks so beautiful, so elegant from behind, turns and shows Ida her ruined and terrifying face. She turns, she looks at Ida, her face is beautiful, composed. A wise, mature face. An ethereal, insightful face. She looks at Ida with turquoise, almond-shaped eyes. It is a greeting from the place where she is headed. Sometimes at night she feels a sudden paralysing pain and hates him. He could ease her pain, her longing. He could have written an ordinary letter, but he doesn't. He could have asked: How are you? Rather than hang up. He could have said: I love you. But I'm married. What are we going to do about our love? But he doesn't.

This is an edited excerpt from If Only *by Vigdis Hjorth (Verso Books, 2024).*

SUNDAY JUNE 1

MONDAY JUNE 2

TUESDAY JUNE 3

JUNE 4, 1450 Jack Cade, who led 5,000 peasants through London, capturing and beheading King Henry VI's associates, issues a manifesto of grievances.

JUNE 4, 1920 The republican-socialist Jangal movement forms the short-lived Persian Soviet Socialist State in the Gilan province of Iran. "By the will of the working people, Soviet power has been organized in Persia." —LETTER TO TROTSKY FROM THE REVOLUTIONARY WAR COUNCIL OF THE PERSIAN RED ARMY

JUNE 4, 1989 As army tanks roll into Beijing's Tiananmen Square, protestors join Hou Dejian in singing his popular song, "Heirs of the Dragon."

"Enemies on all sides, the sword of the dictator.
For how many years did those gunshots resound?"

JUNE 5, 1940 Novelist and Yorkshire radical J. B. Priestley broadcasts his first *Postscript* radio series for the BBC, which drew audiences of up to 16 million listeners, and was soon canceled for being too leftist.

JUNE 5, 2013 The *Guardian* publishes the first batch of government documents leaked by National Security Agency whistle-blower Edward Snowden.

JUNE 7, 1903 James Connolly founds the Socialist Labour Party with comrades in Edinburgh; he is later executed for his role in the Easter Uprising. "Before a shot has been fired by the British army on land, before a battle has been fought at sea, ruin and misery are entering the homes of the working people." —"WAR—WHAT IT MEANS TO YOU"

WEDNESDAY JUNE 4

Lord Saye and Sele Brought Before Jack Cade 4th July 1450
by Charles Lucy

THURSDAY JUNE 5

NOTES:

FRIDAY JUNE 6

SATURDAY JUNE 7

SUNDAY JUNE 8

JUNE 10, 1952 Trinidadian historian, novelist, and critic C. L. R. James is detained at Ellis Island to await deportation from the US. "The African bruises and breaks himself against his bars in the interests of freedoms wider than his own."
—*A HISTORY OF NEGRO REVOLT*

JUNE 10, 1967 The June 1967 War between Israel and Syria, Jordan, and Egypt ends in Arab defeat.

"My grieved country,
In a flash
You changed me from a poet who wrote love
poems
To a poet who writes with a knife."
—SYRIAN POET AND DIPLOMAT NIZAR QABBANI,
"FOOTNOTES TO THE BOOK OF THE SETBACK"

MONDAY JUNE 9

JUNE 12, 1917 Founding of the Liberty League, the first organization of the "New Negro Movement" by Hubert Harrison, a black intellectual and labor leader who immigrated to the US from the US Virgin Islands.

JUNE 13, 1971 The *New York Times* publishes the first of the Daniel Ellsberg-leaked Pentagon Papers, which proved that the US government misled the public on the Vietnam War. "If the war was unjust, as I now regarded it, that meant that every Vietnamese killed by Americans or by the proxies we had financed since the 1950s had been killed by us without justification." —*SECRETS: A MEMOIR OF VIETNAM AND THE PENTAGON PAPERS*

TUESDAY JUNE 10

WEDNESDAY JUNE 11

Trinidadian historian, novelist, and critic C. L. R. James (1901–1989)

THURSDAY JUNE 12

NOTES:

FRIDAY JUNE 13

SATURDAY JUNE 14

SUNDAY JUNE 15

JUNE 15, 1813 Simón Bolívar issues his "Decree of War to the Death" for independence from Spain in Trujillo, Venezuela. "Spaniards and Canarians, count on death, even if indifferent, if you do not actively work in favor of the independence of America. Americans, count on life, even if guilty."

JUNE 15, 2009 Millions take to the streets in the pro-democracy Green Movement in Iran. "My hands and yours, must tear down this curtain." — MANSOUR TEHRANI, "MY GRADE-SCHOOL FRIEND," A 1980S PERSIAN POP SONG THAT BECAME A MOVEMENT ANTHEM

MONDAY JUNE 16

JUNE 16, 1948 The military arm of the Malayan Communist Party fires the first shots of an insurrection against British rule. "Imperialism wants to suppress our struggle for better living conditions with guns and knives and we must answer with more vigorous and larger-scale unified struggle." —EDITORIAL IN PARTY NEWSPAPER MIN SHENG PAO

JUNE 16, 1971 The Polynesian Panther Party is formed in Auckland as a Maori and Pacific Islander civil rights group.

JUNE 18, 1984 British police attack picketing miners with dogs, riot gear, and armored vehicles, in a pivotal event of the 1984–85 UK Miners' Strike. The Battle of Orgreave is believed to be the first use of kettling, the police tactic of deploying a large cordon of officers to surround and entrap protesters.

TUESDAY JUNE 17

JUNE 19, 1977 Ali Shariati, "the ideologue of the Iranian Revolution," is assassinated by the Shah's spies in the UK. "The minds of the people are prepared. The hearts of the enslaved masses are throbbing for revolt under the curtain of secrecy. One spark will be sufficient." —"RED SHI'ISM VS BLACK SHI'ISM"

WEDNESDAY JUNE 18

Ali Shariati (1933-1977) on the Haj

THURSDAY JUNE 19

NOTES:

FRIDAY JUNE 20

SATURDAY JUNE 21

SUNDAY JUNE 22

_____

_____

_____

_____

MONDAY JUNE 23

_____

_____

_____

_____

TUESDAY JUNE 24

_____

_____

_____

_____

_____

_____

JUNE 22, 1955 Historian Eric Williams founds the People's National Movement, which later ushers in independence in Trinidad and Tobago. "The history of our West Indian islands can be expressed in two simple words: Columbus and Sugar." —CAPITALISM AND SLAVERY

JUNE 22, 1897 Indian anticolonialists shoot two British officers, and independence leader Bal Gangadhar Tilak is arrested for incitement. "Swaraj [self-rule] is my birthright and I shall have it!"

JUNE 25, 1876 Battle of Little Bighorn begins in what is now Montana, with combined Lakota, Cheyenne, and Arapaho forces beating the US 7th Cavalry. "I have robbed, killed, and injured too many white men to believe in a good peace. They are medicine, and I would eventually die a lingering death. I would rather die on the field of battle." —NATIVE LEADER SITTING BULL

JUNE 25, 1892 Ida B. Wells, civil rights activist and anti-lynching campaigner, publishes an early version of her pamphlet _Southern Horrors: Lynch Law in All Its Phases_.

JUNE 25, 1962 Mozambique's anticolonial liberation party FRELIMO is founded. In the early 1970s, its guerrilla force of 7,000 fought 60,000 Portuguese colonial troops.

"In our land
bullets are beginning to flower."
—JORGE REBELO, POET BEHIND FRELIMO'S
PROPAGANDA CAMPAIGN

JUNE 28, 1969 Riots begin at New York City's Stonewall Inn in response to a police raid, sparking the modern gay rights movement.

WEDNESDAY JUNE 25

Marsha P. Johnson (1945-1992) and Sylvia Rivera (1951-2002), prominent activists who led the Stonewall Riots

THURSDAY JUNE 26

NOTES:

FRIDAY JUNE 27

SATURDAY JUNE 28

SUNDAY JUNE 29

MONDAY JUNE 30

TUESDAY JULY 1

JUNE 30, 1855 The Santhal Rebellion, led by two brothers, sees peasants across the Bengal Presidency rise up against the British Raj and local landlords.

JULY 2, 1809 Shawnee chief Tecumseh calls on all Indians to unite against the encroachment of white settlers on native land. "The only way to stop this evil is for all the red men to unite in claiming an equal right in the land. That is how it was at first, and should be still, for the land never was divided, but was for the use of everyone." —ADDRESS TO WILLIAM HENRY HARRISON

JULY 4, 1789 The Marquis de Sade is moved from the Bastille prison to Charenton, days before French revolutionaries storm it and set fire to his writings there. "No act of possession can ever be perpetrated on a free being; it is as unjust to own a wife monogamously as it is to own slaves." —PHILOSOPHY IN THE BEDROOM

JULY 4, 1876 Susan B. Anthony and other protesters present the "Declaration of Rights for Women" at an official celebration of the centennial of the United States. "Women's wealth, thought, and labor have cemented the stones of every monument man has reared to liberty."

JULY 4, 1967 The British Parliament decriminalizes homosexuality.

JULY 5, 1885 The Protect the King movement in Vietnam begins, following a French attack on the imperial capital of Hué, and uniting the country against French colonial rule. "Better to be sentenced once than sentenced for eternity." —COORDINATOR OF RESISTANCE IN NORTHERN VIETNAM NGUYỄN QUANG BÍCH, LETTER TO THE FRENCH

WEDNESDAY JULY 2

Design proposal for a US dollar featuring Susan B. Anthony, 1978-1979

THURSDAY JULY 3

NOTES:

FRIDAY JULY 4

SATURDAY JULY 5

SUNDAY JULY 6

MONDAY JULY 7

TUESDAY JULY 8

JULY 7, 1969 Redstockings, a New York–based radical Marxist-feminist group, publishes its manifesto. "Liberated women—very different from women's liberation!" —REDSTOCKINGS MEMBER PAT MAINARDI, "THE POLITICS OF HOUSEWORK"

JULY 9, 1910 Govan Mbeki, leader of the South African Communist Party and the African National Congress, is born. Following the Rivonia Trial, Mbeki served a long-term on Robben Island, during which he managed to run education classes with prisoners, many on Marxist theory, and wrote a number of significant analyses from jail.

JULY 9, 1955 Bertrand Russell and Albert Einstein issue a manifesto condemning the stockpiling and use of nuclear weapons. "There lies before us, if we choose, continual progress in happiness, knowledge, and wisdom. Shall we, instead, choose death, because we cannot forget our quarrels?" —BERTRAND RUSSELL

WEDNESDAY JULY 9

Activists and supporters march outside the Rivonia Trial, 1964

THURSDAY JULY 10

NOTES:

FRIDAY JULY 11

SATURDAY JULY 12

SUNDAY JULY 13

JULY 13, 1934 Nobel Prize-winning Nigerian poet and playwright Wole Soyinka is born. Over the course of his life, Soyinka is prosecuted and jailed numerous times for his outspoken political critiques.

"Traveler you must set forth
At dawn.
I promise marvels of the holy hour."
—"DEATH IN THE DAWN"

JULY 14, 1789 An organized mob breaks into a royal armory in Paris and, newly armed, storms the Bastille, a fortress that held the monarchy's political prisoners. "This very night all the Swiss and German battalions will leave the Champ de Mars to massacre us all. One resource is left; to take arms!" —SPEECH BY JOURNALIST CAMILLE DESMOULINS THAT ROUSED THE PEOPLE THE PREVIOUS DAY

MONDAY JULY 14

JULY 14, 1877 The Great Railroad Strike begins in West Virginia, United States, pitting thousands of railroad workers against state militias and the national guardsmen summoned to break it. "Wages and revenge." —SLOGAN

JULY 18, 1936 Resistance fighter Buenaventura Durruti forms the "Durruti Column," the largest anarchist fighting force in the Spanish Civil War. "The bourgeoisie might blast and ruin its own world before it leaves the stage of history. We carry a new world here, in our hearts." —DURRUTI IN AN INTERVIEW THREE MONTHS BEFORE BEING KILLED

TUESDAY JULY 15

JULY 19, 1961 The Sandinista National Liberation Front (FSLN) is founded; in 1979 it will overthrow the Somoza dictatorship in Nicaragua. "Those of us who propose to wage a struggle to liberate our country and make freedom a reality must rescue our own traditions and put together the facts and figures we need in order to wage an ideological war against our enemy." —FSLN COFOUNDER CARLOS FONSECA, SPEECH IN HAVANA

WEDNESDAY JULY 16

Sandinistas taking a smoke break, 1987

THURSDAY JULY 17

NOTES:

FRIDAY JULY 18

SATURDAY JULY 19

SUNDAY JULY 20

MONDAY JULY 21

TUESDAY JULY 22

JULY 20, 1925 Frantz Fanon, psychiatrist and revolutionary whose writings inspired anticolonial movements throughout the world, is born in Martinique. "HISTORY teaches us clearly that the battle against colonialism does not run straight away along the lines of nationalism." *—THE WRETCHED OF THE EARTH*

JULY 23, 1900 W. E. B. Du Bois attends the First Pan-African Congress in London, where he makes the statement later immortalized in his 1903 book *The Souls of Black Folk*: "The problem of the twentieth century is the problem of the color-line."

JULY 25, 1846 Henry David Thoreau is jailed for refusing to pay taxes due to his opposition to slavery and the Mexican-American War. "Under a government which imprisons any unjustly, the true place for a just man is also a prison." *—CIVIL DISOBEDIENCE*

JULY 26, 1953 Fidel Castro leads the Cuban revolution against the US-backed dictator Fulgencio Batista with an attack on the Moncada Barracks. "Condemn me. It does not matter. History will absolve me." *—CASTRO, BEFORE BEING SENTENCED FOR THE ATTACK*

JULY 26, 1956 Gamal Abdel Nasser, president of Egypt, announces the nationalization of the Suez Canal. "We shall yield neither to force nor the dollar."

WEDNESDAY JULY 23

W. E. B. Du Bois (1868–1963), American sociologist, historian, civil rights activist, Pan-Africanist, author, and editor, in 1918

THURSDAY JULY 24

NOTES:

FRIDAY JULY 25

SATURDAY JULY 26

SOCIAL MEDIA IS A WARZONE:
THE IDF'S STRATEGY FOR WAR AS ONLINE SPECTACLE
ANTONY LOEWENSTEIN

The November 2012 Israeli bombardment of Gaza, called Operation Pillar of Defense, was a seven-day war that killed 174 Palestinians and 6 Israelis and injured thousands more. While the death toll in that operation was relatively low, Israel's Operation Cast Lead in 2008 and early 2009 saw the death of 1,400 Gazans. That conflict saw a revolution in how the IDF portrayed the war across its multiple social media platforms. Worried that public opinion in some Western nations was turning against Israeli military actions, the so-called instawar was a coordinated enterprise to live-tweet military operations and infographics, produced to proudly announce the killing of Hamas members or the arrest of Palestinian "terrorists." These productions sometimes had the feel of a Hollywood-style, big-budget action film.

The Israeli social media strategy aimed to involve both domestic and global supporters of its military missions. By doing so, and asking backers to post their own supporting tweets, Facebook posts, or Instagram images, the IDF created a collective mission that other nations could easily mimic by stirring up nationalist fervor online. During Operation Pillar of Defense, the IDF encouraged supporters of Israel to both proudly share when "terrorists" were killed while at the same time reminding a global audience that the Jewish state was a victim. It was a form of mass conscription to the cause through the weaponization of social media.

This was war as spectacle, and the IDF was spending big to make it happen. The IDF media budget allowed at least 70 officers and 2,000 soldiers to design, process, and disseminate official Israeli propaganda, and almost every social media platform was flooded with IDF content.

Today, the IDF Instagram page regularly features pro-gay and pro-feminist messaging alongside its hard-line militaristic iconography. On October 1, 2021, the IDF posted across its social media platforms a photo of its headquarters swathed in pink light with this message: "For those who are fighting, for those who have passed, and for those who have survived, the IDF HQ is lit up pink this #BreastCancerAwarenessMonth." Palestinian American activist Yousef Munayyer responded on Twitter: "An untold number of women in Gaza suffer from breast cancer and are routinely denied adequate treatment and timely lifesaving care because this military operates a brutal siege

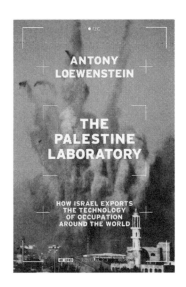

ANTONY LOEWENSTEIN

THE PALESTINE LABORATORY

HOW ISRAEL EXPORTS THE TECHNOLOGY OF OCCUPATION AROUND THE WORLD

The IDF introduced new weapons and paraded them in front of different defense media outlets during the 2014 Gaza war. The technology was profiled, though advertised would be a more accurate term, in Israeli and international media and included bombs, tank shells, and the Elbit Hermes drone. A few weeks after the war ended, the annual Israel Unmanned Systems conference, an event hosted with the US Embassy in Tel Aviv to prospective markets in Asia, Europe, and North and South America, featured some of the weapons used in the Gaza conflict, including the Elbit drone.

The next Israeli experiment was tested in real time during the Great March of Return, when Gazans protested alongside the fence with Israel. Starting in March 2018, it gained massive global attention as Palestinians peacefully demanded an end to the siege on Gaza and the right to return to lands stolen by Israel. Between March 2018 and December 2019, 223 Palestinians were killed, most of whom were civilians, and 8,000 were shot by snipers, some left with life-changing injuries. The IDF tweeted (but then deleted) on March 31: "Yesterday we saw 30,000 people; we arrived prepared and with precise reinforce-ments. Nothing was carried out uncontrolled; everything was accurate and measured, and we know where every bullet landed."

against over 2 million souls." On Instagram, however, most of the comments below the post praised the IDF.

This kind of IDF information war strategy is now routinely copied by the US military. The CIA launched a social media campaign, Humans of CIA, in 2021 that aimed to recruit from more diverse communities into its ranks. It felt deeply inspired by the IDF's woke posturing. One of the most discussed (and mocked) campaigns, considering the CIA's role in destabilizing and overthrowing governments since World War II, was the video of a Latina intelligence officer declaring: "I am a cisgender millennial, who has been diagnosed with generalized anxiety disor-der. I am intersectional, but my existence is not a box-checking exercise. I used to struggle with imposter syndrome, but at thirty-six I refuse to internalize misguided patriarchal ideas of what a woman can or should be."

This is an edited excerpt from The Palestine Laboratory: How Israel Exports the Technology of Occupation Around the World *by Antony Loewenstein (Verso Books, 2023).*

SUNDAY JULY 27

_____

_____

_____

_____

_____

_____

_____

MONDAY JULY 28

_____

_____

_____

_____

_____

_____

TUESDAY JULY 29

_____

_____

_____

_____

_____

_____

JULY 27, 1972 Selma James, cofounder of the International Wages for Housework campaign, and Mariarosa Dalla Costa publish *The Power of Women and the Subversion of the Community*, which identified women's unwaged care work as an essential element of capitalism.

JULY 28, 1794 Maximilien Robespierre, the face of the French Revolution's Reign of Terror, is guillotined without a trial. "The tyrant's trial is insurrection; his judgment is the fall of his power; his penalty, whatever the liberty of the people demands." —"AGAINST GRANTING THE KING A TRIAL"

JULY 29, 1848 The Young Irelander Rebellion of 1848 takes place: a failed Irish nationalist revolt against British rule, sometimes called the Famine Rebellion (since it took place during the Great Irish Famine) or the Battle of Ballingarry.

JULY 31, 1905 The Maji Maji Rebellion begins in what is now Tanzania, led by several tribes in Tanganyika against German colonizers. "Hongo or the European, which is the stronger?" "Hongo!" —REBELLION PASSWORD

AUGUST 1, 1933 Antifascist activists Bruno Tesch, Walter Möller, Karl Wolff, and August Lütgens executed by the Nazi regime in Altona.

AUGUST 2, 1924 James Baldwin, black American novelist, critic, and essayist, is born in Harlem, New York City. "People can cry much easier than they can change, a rule of psychology people like me picked up as kids on the street." —"JAMES BALDWIN BACK HOME"

AUGUST 2, 1997 Fela Kuti, Nigerian father of Afrobeat and frequent presidential candidate, dies from AIDS-related complications.

WEDNESDAY JULY 30

Writer and critic James Baldwin (1924–1987)

THURSDAY JULY 31

NOTES:

FRIDAY AUGUST 1

SATURDAY AUGUST 2

SUNDAY AUGUST 3

MONDAY AUGUST 4

TUESDAY AUGUST 5

AUGUST 3, 1960 Independence Day in the Republic of Niger, marking the nation's independence from France in 1960. Since 1975, it is also Arbor Day, as trees are planted across the nation to aid the fight against desertification.

AUGUST 4, 1983 Revolutionary leader Thomas Sankara assumes power in Burkina Faso, nationalizing mineral wealth and redistributing land. "It took the madmen of yesterday for us to be able to act with extreme clarity today. I want to be one of those madmen. We must dare to invent the future."

AUGUST 5, 1951 Eduardo Chibás, anticommunist Cuban radio personality, shoots himself after his final broadcast. "People of Cuba, keep awake. This is my last knock at your door." —CHIBAS'S LAST WORDS

AUGUST 6, 1969 Theodor Adorno—philosopher, composer, and leading member of the Frankfurt School of critical theory—dies. "For the Enlightenment, anything which cannot be resolved into numbers, and ultimately into one, is illusion; modern positivism consigns it to poetry." —DIALECTIC OF ENLIGHTENMENT, CO-AUTHORED WITH MAX HORKHEIMER

AUGUST 6, 2011 Riots break out throughout London after police kill Mark Duggan, a black man, lasting for several days and leading to more than 3,000 arrests.

AUGUST 8, 1961 Wu Han, a member of a dissident group of Chinese intellectuals, writes a play indirectly critical of Mao and the Great Leap Forward, for which he is imprisoned.

AUGUST 8, 1988 Rangoon students call openly for democracy, sparking the 8888 Uprising that toppled Burma's Ne Win government before being violently crushed by government troops.

WEDNESDAY AUGUST 6

Shop fire in Clapham Junction during the London Riots, August 8, 2011

THURSDAY AUGUST 7

NOTES:

FRIDAY AUGUST 8

SATURDAY AUGUST 9

SUNDAY AUGUST 10

MONDAY AUGUST 11

TUESDAY AUGUST 12

AUGUST 11, 1828 The first Working Men's Party of the United States is founded in Philadelphia. "And for the support of this declaration, we mutually pledge to each other our faithful aid to the end of our lives." —GEORGE HENRY EVANS, "PARTY DECLARATION OF INDEPENDENCE"

AUGUST 14, 1980 Polish shipyard workers strike to protest the firing of worker Anna Walentynowicz and for the right to form unions. Walentynowicz is reinstated, and several weeks later, the first independent labor union in a Soviet bloc country, Solidarność, is formed, precipitating the fall of the Polish communist regime. "It was the end of the utopian dream, and it enabled us to dismantle the dictatorship by negotiation." —ACTIVIST ADAM MICHNIK

AUGUST 15, 1947 India becomes independent after 200 years of British colonial rule. "A moment comes, which comes but rarely in history, when we step out from the old to the new, when an age ends, and when the soul of a nation, long suppressed, finds utterance." —MOVEMENT LEADER AND INDIA'S FIRST PRIME MINISTER JAWAHARLAL NEHRU, "TRYST WITH DESTINY"

AUGUST 16, 1819 The English cavalry charges into a crowd of over 60,000 rallying in Manchester for parliamentary reform in what becomes known as the Peterloo Massacre.

"Rise like lions after slumber
In unvanquishable number—
Shake your chains to earth like dew
Which in sleep had fallen on you—
Ye are many—they are few!"
　　　—PERCY BYSSHE SHELLEY'S "THE MASQUE OF ANARCHY,"
　　　AN EARLY STATEMENT OF NONVIOLENT RESISTANCE

WEDNESDAY AUGUST 13

A painting of the Peterloo Massacre circulated in pro-suffrage papers, 1819

THURSDAY AUGUST 14

NOTES:

FRIDAY AUGUST 15

SATURDAY AUGUST 16

SUNDAY AUGUST 17

MONDAY AUGUST 18

TUESDAY AUGUST 19

AUGUST 18, 1914 Mekatilili Wa Menza, leader of the Kenyan Giriama people against the British Colonial Administration from 1913 to 1914, dies. "And Champion took a chick and the hen flapped and attacked him. And the Giriama said, you see what this hen has done? If you take our sons, we will do the same." —GIRIAMA TALE, IN WHICH MEKATILILI IS PERSONIFIED AS THE HEN

AUGUST 19, 1953 Mohammad Mosaddegh, the popular, democratically elected prime minister of Iran, is overthrown by a CIA-backed coup. "My greatest sin is that I nationalized Iran's oil industry and discarded the system of political and economic exploitation by the world's greatest empire." —SPEECH AT HIS TRIAL

AUGUST 21, 1791 A rebellion against slavery breaks out in Saint-Domingue, leading to the Haitian Revolution, the only slave revolt against European colonialists that successfully achieved an independent state. "We seek only to bring men to the liberty that God has given them, and that other men have taken from them only by transgressing His immutable will." —REVOLUTIONARY LEADER TOUSSAINT L'OUVERTURE

AUGUST 21, 1940 Leon Trotsky, Marxist revolutionary and theorist, is assassinated by Soviet agents. "Life is beautiful. Let the future generations cleanse it of all evil, oppression and violence, and enjoy it to the full." —"TROTSKY'S TESTAMENT," WRITTEN MONTHS EARLIER

AUGUST 23, 1927 During the Red Scare—a period of intense political repression in the US—the Italian-born anarchists Nicola Sacco and Bartolomeo Vanzetti are wrongfully convicted and executed for robbery and murder.

WEDNESDAY AUGUST 20

Attack and taking of the Crête-à-Pierrot, illustration by Auguste Raffet, 1839

THURSDAY AUGUST 21

NOTES:

FRIDAY AUGUST 22

SATURDAY AUGUST 23

SUNDAY AUGUST 24

MONDAY AUGUST 25

TUESDAY AUGUST 26

AUGUST 25, 1968 Yippies—the Youth International Party, which brought counterculture theatricality to the US antiwar and New Left movements—host their Festival of Life at the Democratic National Convention in Chicago, leading to police actions and a trial for conspiracy to riot for the organizers. "There will be public fornication whenever and wherever there is an aroused appendage and willing apertures." —ACTIVIST ED SANDERS, "PREDICTIONS FOR YIPPIE ACTIVITIES"

AUGUST 26, 1789 The "Declaration of the Rights of Man and of the Citizen"—a document of the French Revolution and civil rights—is adopted by the National Constituent Assembly in France. Nicolas de Condorcet, Etta Palm d'Aelders, and Olympe de Gouges called for these rights to be extended to women; Vincent Ogé, following the Haitian Revolution of 1791-1804, attempted to extend them to men of color and then to slaves.

AUGUST 29, 1786 Poor farmers crushed by debt and taxes rise up in armed rebellion in Massachusetts, US, in what came to be known as Shay's Rebellion. "The great men are going to get all we have and I think it is time for us to rise and put a stop to it, and have no more courts, nor sheriffs, nor collectors, nor lawyers." —PLOUGH JOGGER, FARMER, SPEAKING AT THE ILLEGAL CONVENTION OPPOSING THE MASSACHUSETTS LEGISLATURE

AUGUST 29, 1844 Edward Carpenter, pioneering socialist poet, philosopher, and early homosexual thinker, is born in England. "It has become clear that the number of individuals affected with 'sexual inversion' in some degree or other is very great—much greater than is generally supposed to be the case." —HOMOGENIC LOVE

WEDNESDAY AUGUST 27

Declaration of the Rights of Man and of the Citizen, painted by Jean-Jacques-François Le Barbier

THURSDAY AUGUST 28

NOTES:

FRIDAY AUGUST 29

SATURDAY AUGUST 30

THE POLITICS OF NEURODIVERSITY
JODIE HARE

As an increasing number of diagnoses are made and more people come to understand themselves as neurodivergent, we cannot just accept that huge numbers of people should live with such a low quality of life. It matters to me that neurodivergent people know they have as much of a right to a long, happy life as anyone else, and that they feel this view is reflected in the society they live in.

Forging a world where neurodivergent individuals are safe and supported requires the erasure of systemic injustices that also impact marginalised groups affected by discrimination based on disability, class, race, gender, sexuality, and more. However, even as we gain a better understanding of it, the concept of neurodiversity is in the process of being watered down. The word is being stripped of its political potential. Neurodivergence is increasingly seen as a marketable attribute.

Companies are beginning to ask how they might use neurodivergent workers to increase profit margins. *Harvard Business Review* printed articles with titles like "Neurodiversity Is a Competitive Advantage," concluding that "the potential returns are great" and that managers should "do the hard work of fitting irregular puzzle pieces together" (the "irregular" pieces of course being the neurodivergent individuals themselves). Others believe that the term "neurodiversity" is gaining traction because it is "preferable to 'disability' or words with a similarly negative connotation." This use of neurodiversity as a euphemism is rooted in ableism. It suggests that the word "disability" should be avoided at all costs, that it is something to be ashamed of, or that there is something about attaching it to your personhood that is undesirable.

As well as failing to capture the aims of the campaign, this co-optation of "neurodiversity" insinuates that those invested in the campaign are ashamed of the word "disability"—which is also untrue. As an autistic person who believes in the values at the heart of the neurodiversity campaign, this saddens me. Neurodiversity is one stepping stone along a road filled with opportunities for positive social change, and I do not want this political potential to be overlooked.

Many thinkers over the years have explained how societal systems are strengthened and maintained through the oppression of marginalised groups. Angela Davis has explained that racism will not be eradicated without the eradication of racial capitalism, while others have discussed how homophobia cannot thrive without the workings of the patriarchy—and the list goes on. Making changes to our society in the name of neurodiversity requires us to fix some of our wider issues with discrimination and poverty, while also thinking about access to health care, education, and much more.

Understanding neurodiversity as a political campaign inherently linked to every other cause for liberation means widening the net. It requires us to forge connections across various struggles and ask how solving one issue might offer a solution to others. Marta Rose, a neurodivergent writer and artist, remarks on her Instagram: "There is no liberation for neurodivergent people that doesn't float on a river moving

Jodie Hare

Autism is Not a Disease

The Politics of Neurodiversity

all peoples and creatures towards freedom." This statement, as well as its inverse—that the liberation of all will not occur without liberation from neuronormativity—speaks to the core tenet of my work. The neurodiversity movement is an ever-growing part of a disability-informed battle for justice and equality.

*

Thanks to the size of the neurodiversity community and the number of competing ideas within it, there are, quite rightly, no clearly defined rules for who can now be considered neurodivergent, and many debates have been conducted about who should be included. What makes the many diagnoses significant is their ability to shape who a person is at their core. Unlike diagnoses of temporary or curable conditions, these affect the way a person interprets the world around them, how they process outside information and how they exist in the world. An often-cited quote from Jim Sinclair, one of the founding members of the Autism Network International, reads:

> Autism isn't something a person has, or a "shell" that a person is trapped inside. There's no normal child hidden behind the autism. Autism is a way of being. It is pervasive; it colors every experience, every sensation, perception, thought, emotion, and encounter, every aspect of existence. It is not possible to separate the autism from the person—and if it were possible, the person you'd have left would not be the same person you started with.

This is an edited excerpt from Autism Is Not a Disease: The Politics of Neurodiversity *by Jodie Hare (Verso Books, 2024).*

SUNDAY AUGUST 31

MONDAY SEPTEMBER 1

TUESDAY SEPTEMBER 2

SEPTEMBER 1, 1961 The Eritrean struggle for independence begins when members of the Eritrean Liberation Front fire first shots on the occupying Ethiopian army.

"What have I done
That you deny me my torch?"
—"SHIGEY HABUNI," POPULAR SONG WITH TIES TO THE NATIONALIST MOVEMENT

SEPTEMBER 2, 1945 Following two weeks of insurgency against French colonial forces, Ho Chi Minh and the Viet Minh seize control of the country and declare Vietnam independent. "Poor Indochina! You will die, if your old-fashioned youth do not resuscitate themselves." —HO CHI MINH PAMPHLET THAT BECAME THE "BIBLE OF NATIONALISTS" TWO DECADES LATER

SEPTEMBER 3, 2017 Private security guards for the Dakota Access Pipeline unleash dogs on indigenous water protectors near the Standing Rock Sioux Tribe reservation in North Dakota. A protest encampment, established months earlier, quickly swelled to become the largest gathering of Native Americans in recent history. "Mní Wičoni—Water Is Life." —SLOGAN

SEPTEMBER 6, 1960 "Manifesto of the 121" is signed by French intellectuals (including Jean-Paul Sartre, Maurice Blanchot, and others), supporting the right of Algerians to fight for independence from the French. "Must we be reminded that fifteen years after the destruction of the Hitlerite order, French militarism has managed to bring back torture and restore it as an institution in Europe?"

WEDNESDAY SEPTEMBER 3

Ho Chi Minh (1890–1969) with East German sailors in Stralsund Harbor, 1957

THURSDAY SEPTEMBER 4

NOTES:

FRIDAY SEPTEMBER 5

SATURDAY SEPTEMBER 6

SUNDAY SEPTEMBER 7

MONDAY SEPTEMBER 8

TUESDAY SEPTEMBER 9

SEPTEMBER 7, 1872 Russian revolutionary and anarchist theorist Mikhail Bakunin is expelled from the First International, presaging a split between the anarchist and Marxist factions of the workers' movement. "If you took the most ardent revolutionary, vested him in absolute power, within a year he would be worse than the Tsar himself." —BAKUNIN ON AUTHORITARIAN SOCIALISM

SEPTEMBER 8, 1965 Delano Grape Strike begins in California when Filipino grape pickers walk out and ask Cesar Chavez, leader of the mostly Latino National Farm Workers Association, to join them. The campaign ended five years later in success, largely due to a consumer boycott. "Time accomplishes for the poor what money does for the rich." —CHAVEZ, "LETTER FROM DELANO"

SEPTEMBER 9, 869 Ali ibn Muhammad, a leader of the Zanj uprising of African slaves against the Abbasid Caliphate in Iraq, begins freeing slaves and gaining adherents. "Ali ordered their slaves to bring whips of palm branches and, while their masters and agents were prostrated on the ground, each one was given five hundred lashes." —PERSIAN HISTORIAN IBN JARIR AL-TABARI

SEPTEMBER 9, 1739 Stono Rebellion, the largest slave uprising in Britain's mainland North American colonies, led by a slave called Jemmy, erupts near Charleston, South Carolina. Over the next two years, slave uprisings occurred independently in Georgia and South Carolina.

SEPTEMBER 11, 1973 Salvador Allende, socialist president of Chile, bids farewell to the nation as US-backed General Pinochet carries out a coup d'état. "I will pay for [my] loyalty to the people with my life. And I say to them that I am certain that the seeds which we have planted in the good conscience of thousands and thousands of Chileans will not be shriveled forever."

WEDNESDAY SEPTEMBER 10

Cesar Chavez (1927-1993) following the successful farmworker strike and consumer grape boycott, 1970

THURSDAY SEPTEMBER 11

NOTES:

FRIDAY SEPTEMBER 12

SATURDAY SEPTEMBER 13

SUNDAY SEPTEMBER 14

MONDAY SEPTEMBER 15

TUESDAY SEPTEMBER 16

SEPTEMBER 14, 1791 Olympe de Gouges publishes the *Declaration of the Rights of Women and the Female Citizen,* one of the first tracts to champion women's rights. "Woman is born free and remains the equal of man in rights."

SEPTEMBER 15, 1889 Claude McKay, Harlem Renaissance poet and delegate to the Third International, is born in Jamaica.

SEPTEMBER 16, 1810 Miguel Hidalgo, a priest in Dolores, Mexico, issues a call to revolt against Spanish rule, setting in motion the Mexican War of Independence. "My children: a new dispensation comes to us today. Will you receive it? Will you free yourselves?"

SEPTEMBER 16, 1923 Alongside her lover and his six-year-old nephew, Ito Noe, anarchist and feminist writer and activist, is brutally murdered by Japanese police. The event, known as the Amakasu Incident, sparked outrage throughout Japan and led to a ten-year sentence for the officer.

SEPTEMBER 16, 1973 Victor Jara, Chilean poet and songwriter, is tortured and killed in Chile Stadium following Pinochet's coup against Allende.

"How hard is it to sing
when I must sing of horror"

—"ESTADIO CHILE," WRITTEN BY JARA IN THE STADIUM
AND SMUGGLED OUT INSIDE A SHOE

SEPTEMBER 19, 1921 The Brazilian educator and philosopher Paulo Freire is born. His *Pedagogy of the Oppressed* infuses a classical theory of education with Marxist and anticolonialist approaches. "This, then, is the great humanistic and historical task of the oppressed: to liberate themselves and their oppressors as well."

WEDNESDAY SEPTEMBER 17

Ito Noe (1895–1923), Japanese anarchist and feminist

THURSDAY SEPTEMBER 18

NOTES:

FRIDAY SEPTEMBER 19

SATURDAY SEPTEMBER 20

SUNDAY SEPTEMBER 21

MONDAY SEPTEMBER 22

TUESDAY SEPTEMBER 23

SEPTEMBER 21, 1956 Nicaraguan poet Rigoberto López Pérez assassinates Anastasio Somoza García, the longtime dictator of Nicaragua, before being killed himself. "Seeing that all efforts to return Nicaragua to being (or to becoming for the first time) a free country without shame or stain have been futile, I have decided that I should be the one to try to initiate the beginning of the end of this tyranny." —LETTER TO HIS MOTHER

SEPTEMBER 23, 1884 Liberal party partisans occupy a mountaintop in Kabasan, Japan, in a rebellion against the Meiji government.

"Yet while we lament, asking
why our insignificant selves
were oppressed,
the rain still falls
heavily on the people."
—PARTICIPANT OHASHI GENZABURO

SEPTEMBER 23, 1973 Pablo Neruda, Chilean poet and Nobel Prize winner, is poisoned by Pinochet's regime and dies. "When the trumpet blared everything on earth was prepared and Jehovah distributed the world to Coca-Cola Inc., Anaconda, Ford Motors and other entities: the United Fruit Inc. reserved for itself the juiciest, the central seaboard of my land, America's sweet waist." —"UNITED FRUIT CO."

SEPTEMBER 24, 1838 A meeting held on Kersal Moor in England launches the Chartist movement, the first mass working-class movement in Europe.

SEPTEMBER 26, 1940 Fleeing Vichy France, Marxist theorist Walter Benjamin is threatened with deportation from Spain and kills himself with morphine tablets.

WEDNESDAY SEPTEMBER 24

Pablo Neruda (1904–1973) recording his poetry at the US
Library of Congress in 1966

THURSDAY SEPTEMBER 25

NOTES:

FRIDAY SEPTEMBER 26

SATURDAY SEPTEMBER 27

SUNDAY SEPTEMBER 28

MONDAY SEPTEMBER 29

TUESDAY SEPTEMBER 30

SEPTEMBER 1875 Senator William Allison arrives in Sioux country to negotiate a land lease agreement with the Native Americans that would have allowed the United States government to mine the area for gold. His proposal is met with 300 mounted warriors, led by Little Big Man, who chant the song below in response.

"The Black Hills is my land and I love it
And whoever interferes
Will hear this gun."
—SIOUX WARRIORS' SONG

SEPTEMBER 28, 1829 David Walker, a contributor to the first African American newspaper *Freedom Journal*, publishes his *Appeal to the Colored Citizens of the World*, calling for slaves to revolt against their masters. Southern plantation owners respond by putting a $3,000 bounty on his head. "The whites want slaves, and want us for their slaves, but some of them will curse the day they ever saw us."

SEPTEMBER 30, 1935 The anti-Stalinist Workers' Party of Marxist Unification (POUM) is founded in Spain, where it is especially active during the Civil War. "The totalitarian states can do great things, but there is one thing they cannot do: they cannot give the factory-worker a rifle and tell him to take it home and keep it in his bedroom. That rifle hanging on the wall of the working-class flat or laborer's cottage is the symbol of democracy."
—POUM MEMBER GEORGE ORWELL, ARTICLE IN THE *EVENING STANDARD*

OCTOBER 1, 1949 Mao Zedong establishes the People's Republic of China. "A revolution is not a dinner party, or writing an essay, or painting a picture, or doing embroidery; it cannot be so refined, so leisurely and gentle, so temperate, kind, courteous, restrained and magnanimous." —"REPORT ON AN INVESTIGATION OF THE PEASANT MOVEMENT IN HUNAN"

WEDNESDAY OCTOBER 1

Little Big Man—an Oglala Lakota, or Oglala Sioux, leader

THURSDAY OCTOBER 2

NOTES:

FRIDAY OCTOBER 3

SATURDAY OCTOBER 4

SUNDAY OCTOBER 5

MONDAY OCTOBER 6

TUESDAY OCTOBER 7

OCTOBER 5, 1877 Nez Perce leader Hinmatóowy-alahtq'it, also known as Chief Joseph, ends a legendary three-month flight to Canada by surrendering to US forces. "Do not misunderstand me, but understand fully with reference to my affection for the land. I never said the land was mine to do with as I choose. The one who has a right to dispose of it is the one who created it."

OCTOBER 5, 1959 Robert F. Williams's Black Armed Guard fires on Ku Klux Klan members riding past a member's house in North Carolina. "Nowhere in the annals of history does the record show a people delivered from bondage by patience alone." —"WE MUST FIGHT BACK"

OCTOBER 7, 1979 Landless farmers occupy the Macali land in Ronda Alta, Brazil, leading to the founding of the Landless Workers Movement (MST). "This is what I've always wanted: 'to overcome, to overcome.'" —MST LEADER MIGUEL ALVES DOS SANTOS

OCTOBER 10, 1911 The Wuchang Uprising begins after the Qing government suppresses political protest against the handover of local railways to foreign ventures. Quickly spreading through China, the Xinhai Revolution took down the 2,100-year-old dynastic empire within months.

OCTOBER 10, 1947 Senegalese railway workers begin a strike that lasted months, in what would become a watershed moment in Senegal's anticolonial struggle. "It rolled out over its own length, like the movement of a serpent. It was as long as a life." —GOD'S BITS OF WOOD, A NOVEL BY FILMMAKER, WRITER, AND ACTIVIST OUSMANE SEMBÈNE BASED ON THE STRIKE

WEDNESDAY OCTOBER 8

The two flags of the Wuchang Uprising at the birth of the Republic of China

THURSDAY OCTOBER 9

NOTES:

FRIDAY OCTOBER 10

SATURDAY OCTOBER 11

SUNDAY OCTOBER 12

MONDAY OCTOBER 13

TUESDAY OCTOBER 14

OCTOBER 15, 1966 The Black Panther Party is founded in Oakland, California. "The people never make revolution. The oppressors by their brutal actions cause the resistance by the people. The vanguard party only teaches the correct methods of resistance." —COFOUNDER HUEY P. NEWTON, "THE CORRECT HANDLING OF A REVOLUTION"

OCTOBER 15, 1968 The Jamaican government bans the Guyanese scholar and Black Power activist Walter Rodney from the country, sparking what became known as the Rodney Riots. "The only great men among the unfree and the oppressed are those who struggle to destroy the oppressor." —HOW EUROPE UNDERDEVELOPED AFRICA

OCTOBER 17, 1961 Algerian demonstrators in Paris, denouncing France's colonial war in their home country, are met with force. An estimated 300 were massacred; the French government acknowledges forty victims.

OCTOBER 18, 1899 The Battle of Senluo Temple breaks out in northern China between government forces and the Militia United in Righteousness—known in English as the "Boxers" for their strict martial arts regimen—in what would eventually become the Boxer Rebellion, an anti-foreign and anti-Christian uprising.

"When at last all the Foreign Devils
 are expelled to the very last man,
 The Great Qing, united, together,
 will bring peace to this our land"
  —BOXERS WALL POSTER

WEDNESDAY OCTOBER 15

A Chinese "Boxer," 1900

THURSDAY OCTOBER 16

NOTES:

FRIDAY OCTOBER 17

SATURDAY OCTOBER 18

SUNDAY OCTOBER 19

_____

_____

_____

_____

_____

MONDAY OCTOBER 20

_____

_____

_____

_____

_____

_____

_____

TUESDAY OCTOBER 21

_____

_____

_____

_____

_____

_____

OCTOBER 19, 1986 Samora Machel, Mozambican revolutionary leader and post-independence president, dies in a plane crash in South Africa.

OCTOBER 21, 1956 Dedan Kimathi, leader of Kenya's Mau Mau Uprising, is captured by a British colonial officer later nicknamed the "Butcher of Bahrain." "I lead them because God never created any nation to be ruled by another nation forever."

OCTOBER 22, 1964 Jean-Paul Sartre refuses to accept the Nobel Prize for Literature. "The writer must therefore refuse to let himself be transformed into an institution." —LETTER TO THE NOBEL COMMITTEE

OCTOBER 23, 1850 First National Women's Rights Convention meets in Worcester, Massachusetts. The following year, poet and journalist Elizabeth Oakes Smith is nominated as its president, only to be rejected after showing up in a dress baring her neck and arms. "Do we fully understand that we aim at nothing less than an entire subversion of the existing order of society, a dissolution of the whole existing social compact?"

OCTOBER 23, 1856 Du Wenxiu is named Leader of All Muslims in the state established by the Panthay Rebellion, a separatist movement of the Muslim Hui people in southern China.

"They fleece sums of money,
They turn nice scenery into hell.
Alongside of extracting the land tax,
They scrape from the earth even its skin."
—DU WENXIU, WALL POSTER

WEDNESDAY OCTOBER 22

Portrait of Elizabeth Oakes Smith (1806–1893), c. 1845, by John Wesley Paradise

THURSDAY OCTOBER 23

NOTES:

FRIDAY OCTOBER 24

SATURDAY OCTOBER 25

AL RABWEH
JOHN BERGER

A few days after our return from what was thought of, until recently, as the future state of Palestine, and which is now the world's largest prison (Gaza) and the world's largest waiting room (the West Bank), I had a dream.

I was alone, standing, stripped to the waist, in a sandstone desert. Eventually somebody else's hand scooped up some dusty soil from the ground and threw it at my chest. It was a considerate rather than an aggressive act. The soil or gravel changed, before it touched me, into torn strips of cloth, probably cotton, which wrapped themselves around my torso. Then these tattered rags changed again and became words, phrases. Written not by me but by the place. Remembering this dream, the invented word *landswept* came to my mind. Repeatedly. Landswept describes a place or places where everything, both material and immaterial, has been brushed aside, purloined, swept away, blown down, irrigated off, everything except the touchable earth.

There's a small hill called Al Rabweh on the western outskirts of Ramallah, it's at the end of Tokyo street. Near the top of this hill the poet Mahmoud Darwish is buried. It's not a cemetery. The street is named Tokyo because it leads to the city's Cultural Centre, which is at the foot of the hill, and was built thanks to Japanese funding. It was in this Centre that Darwish read some of his poems for the last time—though no one then supposed it would be the last. What does the word *last* mean in moments of desolation?

We went to visit the grave. There's a headstone. The dug earth is still bare, and mourners have left on it little sheaves of green wheat—as he suggested in one of his poems. There are also red anemones, scraps of paper, photos.

He wanted to be buried in Galilee where he was born and where his mother still lives, but the Israelis forbade it.

At the funeral tens of thousands of people assembled here, at Al Rabweh. His mother, years old, addressed them. "He is the son of you all," she said.

On the now deserted hill I tried to recall Darwish's voice. He had the calm voice of a beekeeper:

Mural
Mahmoud Darwish

Translated by John Berger and Rema Hammami

It's no longer possible to squat beside him. His words, however, are audible to our ears and will remain so and we can repeat them.

> I have work to do on the geography
>   of volcanoes
> From desolation to ruin
> from the time of Lot to Hiroshima
> As if I'd never yet lived
> with a lust I've still to know
> Perhaps Now has gone further away
> and yesterday come closer
> So I take Now's hand to walk along the
>   hem of history
> and avoid cyclic time
> with its chaos of mountain goats
> How can my tomorrow be saved?
> By the velocity of electronic time
> or by my desert caravan slowness?
> I have work till my end
> as if I won't see tomorrow
> and I have work for today who isn't here
> So I listen
> softly softly
> to the ant beat of my heart ...

A box of stone
where the living and dead move
    in the dry clay
like bees captive in a honeycomb
    in a hive
and each time the siege tightens
they go on a flower hunger strike
and ask the sea to indicate the
    emergency exit.

Recalling his voice, I felt the need to sit down on the touchable earth, on the green grass. I did so. Al Rabweh means in Arabic: "the hill with green grass on it." His words have returned to where they came from.

*

Mahmoud Darwish's grave on the hill of Al Rabweh has now, following decisions made by the Palestinian Authority, been fenced off, and a glass pyramid has been constructed over it.

Ramallah and Haute Savoie
Early autumn, 2008
John Berger

This is an edited excerpt from the introduction to Mural *by Mahmoud Darwish. Translated by John Berger and Rema Hammami (republished by Verso Books, 2024).*

SUNDAY OCTOBER 26

MONDAY OCTOBER 27

TUESDAY OCTOBER 28

OCTOBER 27, 1967 The 1967 Abortion Act was passed in the United Kingdom, legalizing abortions for up to twenty-eight weeks. Women in Northern Ireland continue to be excluded from access to this health care in their own country.

OCTOBER 28, 1647 The Putney Debates begin, in which members of the New Model Army, who had recently seized London, debate Britain's new constitution. "The poorest man in England is not bound in a strict sense to that government that he hath not had a voice to put himself under." —LEVELLERS SUPPORTER COLONEL RAINSBOROUGH ARGU-ING FOR UNIVERSAL MALE SUFFRAGE

OCTOBER 29, 1888 Li Dazhao, librarian, intel-lectual, and cofounder of the Chinese Commu-nist Party, is born. "China is a rural nation and most of the laboring class consists of peasants. Unless they are liberated, our whole nation will not be liberated." —"DEVELOP THE PEASANTRY"

OCTOBER 29, 1956 Israel invades Egypt after its nationalization of the Suez Canal, followed a few days later by UK and French troops; they are met with local resistance.

OCTOBER 30, 1969 The Kenya People's Union is banned, transforming the country into a one-party state; its leader, the Luo chief and first vice president of independent Kenya Oginga Odinga, is detained. "We fought for *uhuru* so that people may rule themselves. Direct action, not underhand diplomacy and silent intrigue by professional politicians, won *uhuru*, and only popular mobilization can make it meaningful." —*NOT YET UHURU*

WEDNESDAY OCTOBER 29

Chinese comintern Li Dazhao (1888-1927)

THURSDAY OCTOBER 30

NOTES:

FRIDAY OCTOBER 31

SATURDAY NOVEMBER 1

SUNDAY NOVEMBER 2

MONDAY NOVEMBER 3

TUESDAY NOVEMBER 4

NOVEMBER 1811 A letter sent from "Ned Ludd" in Nottingham, England, threatens to break the looms of a property owner, in an early document from the Luddite Uprising.

"The guilty may fear but no vengeance he aims
At the honest man's life or Estate"
—LUDDITES, "GENERAL LUDDS TRIUMPH"

NOVEMBER 4, 1780 Quechua leader Túpac Amaru II leads an indigenous rebellion against Spanish control of Peru, beginning with the capture and killing of the Spanish governor by his slave.

NOVEMBER 7, 1917 Lenin leads the Bolsheviks in revolution against the provisional Russian government, establishing what will become the Soviet Union. "Freedom in capitalist society always remains about the same as it was in the ancient Greek republics: freedom for the slave-owners."
—THE STATE AND REVOLUTION

NOVEMBER 8, 1775 Thomas Spence, English radical and advocate for common ownership of land, delivers a speech with one of the earliest uses of the term "Rights of Man."

"Ye landlords vile, whose man's peace mar,
Come levy rents here if you can;
Your stewards and lawyers I defy,
And live with all the RIGHTS OF MAN"

NOVEMBER 8, 1926 Antonio Gramsci, leader of the Italian Communist Party, is arrested by Mussolini and sentenced to twenty years in prison, during which time he would write his famous *Prison Notebooks*. "'Vanguards' without armies to back them up, 'commandos' without infantry or artillery, these too are transpositions from the language of rhetorical heroism." —"VOLUNTARISM AND SOCIAL MASSES"

WEDNESDAY NOVEMBER 5

Lenin (1870-1924) speaking at an assembly of Red Army troops
bound for the Polish front, with Trotsky at the base, Moscow, 1920

THURSDAY NOVEMBER 6

NOTES:

FRIDAY NOVEMBER 7

SATURDAY NOVEMBER 8

SUNDAY NOVEMBER 9

MONDAY NOVEMBER 10

TUESDAY NOVEMBER 11

NOVEMBER 10, 1995 Nigerian government hangs Ken Saro-Wiwa and the rest of the Ogoni Nine for their campaigning against the oil industry, and especially Royal Dutch Shell. "Dance your anger and your joys; dance the military guns to silence; dance their dumb laws to the dump; dance oppression and injustice to death; dance the end of Shell's ecological war of thirty years."
—STATEMENT OF THE OGONI PEOPLE TO THE TENTH SESSION OF THE WORKING GROUP IN INDIGENOUS POPULATIONS

NOVEMBER 12, 1798 Father of Irish republicanism Wolfe Tone was to be executed by the British for treason, but slit his own throat before the sentence was carried out.

NOVEMBER 13, 1787 Thomas Jefferson, slaveholder and author of the American Declaration of Independence, endorses frequent rebellion in a letter to William Smith. "What signify a few lives lost in a century or two? The tree of liberty must be refreshed from time to time with the blood of patriots and tyrants. It is its natural manure."

NOVEMBER 13, 1792 Louis Antoine de Saint-Just, close friend and ally of Robespierre, delivers his first speech to the revolutionary National Convention in favor of executing the king. "Dare! The word contains all the politics of our revolution."

NOVEMBER 15, 1781 Túpac Katari, Aymara leader of an army that laid siege to the Spanish colonial city of La Paz, Bolivia, is betrayed and killed. "I die but will return tomorrow as thousand thousands."
—KATARI'S LAST WORDS

NOVEMBER 15, 1988 Palestinian Declaration of Independence, written by poet Mahmoud Darwish, is proclaimed.

"O those who pass between fleeting words
Pile your illusions in a deserted pit, and be gone"

WEDNESDAY NOVEMBER 12

The leadership of the PLO during their confrontation with the King of Jordan, 1970

THURSDAY NOVEMBER 13

NOTES:

FRIDAY NOVEMBER 14

SATURDAY NOVEMBER 15

SUNDAY NOVEMBER 16

_____

_____

_____

_____

_____

_____

_____

MONDAY NOVEMBER 17

_____

_____

_____

_____

_____

_____

TUESDAY NOVEMBER 18

_____

_____

_____

_____

_____

_____

NOVEMBER 16, 1885 Louis Riel, Métis leader who headed two rebellions against a Canadian incursion into their territory, is hanged for treason. "I will perhaps be one day acknowledged as more than a leader of the half-breeds, and if I am I will have an opportunity of being acknowledged as a leader of good in this great country." —RIEL'S FINAL STATEMENT TO THE JURY

NOVEMBER 19, 1915 Joe Hill, militant songwriter and organizer with the International Workers of the World, is executed by firing squad. "Don't waste any time in mourning—organize." —HILL'S FAREWELL LETTER TO BILL HAYWOOD

NOVEMBER 19, 1979 Angela Davis—black feminist, philosopher, and prison abolitionist—wins the vice presidential nomination for the US Communist Party. "Prisons do not disappear problems, they disappear human beings. And the practice of disappearing vast numbers of people from poor, immigrant, and racially marginalized communities has literally become big business." —"MASKED RACISM"

NOVEMBER 20, 1969 The Native American group Indians of All Tribes occupies Alcatraz Island in the San Francisco Bay and holds it for fourteen months. "Alcatraz Island is more than suitable as an Indian Reservation, as determined by the white man's own standards." —ALCATRAZ PROCLAMATION

WEDNESDAY NOVEMBER 19

Angela Davis on her first visit to the Soviet Union, 1972

THURSDAY NOVEMBER 20

NOTES:

FRIDAY NOVEMBER 21

SATURDAY NOVEMBER 22

SUNDAY NOVEMBER 23

MONDAY NOVEMBER 24

TUESDAY NOVEMBER 25

NOVEMBER 24, 1947 House Un-American Activities Committee votes to hold the "Hollywood Ten," a group of writers and directors blacklisted for their communist affiliations, in contempt of Congress.

NOVEMBER 24, 2014 A white police officer is acquitted in the shooting death of an unarmed black teenager, Michael Brown, in Ferguson, Missouri, setting off protests nationwide under the moniker Black Lives Matter.

NOVEMBER 25, 1832 Abd al-Qader al-Jaza'iri, Sufi and Muslim scholar and Algerian resistance leader, is elected emir of a confederation of tribes that banded together and fought the French invaders for over a decade.

NOVEMBER 25, 1911 Mexican revolutionary Emiliano Zapata proclaims his Plan de Ayala, laying out his ideology and program of land reform, whose slogan "Land and Freedom!" was a watchword of the Mexican Revolution. "The nation is tired of false men and traitors who make promises like liberators and who on arriving in power forget them and constitute themselves as tyrants."

NOVEMBER 29, 1947 The UN approves the partition of Palestine, despite its rejection by Palestinian Arabs and the fact that 90 percent of privately held land was Arab-owned.

"They've prohibited oppression among
   themselves
but for us they legalized all prohibitions!
They proclaim, 'Trading with slaves is unlawful'
but isn't the trading of free people more
   of a crime?"
   —PALESTINIAN POET ABU SALMA, "MY COUNTRY
   ON PARTITION DAY"

WEDNESDAY NOVEMBER 26

Black Lives Matter protest against police brutality, 2015

THURSDAY NOVEMBER 27

NOTES:

FRIDAY NOVEMBER 28

SATURDAY NOVEMBER 29

V

JOURNEY TO RAMALLAH
GHADA KARMI

"What the hell was I thinking of?"

I had sworn never to return to this torn-up, unhappy land after that first trip in 1991 when I broke a long-standing family taboo against ever visiting the place that had been Palestine and then became Israel. It had always been too painful to contemplate, too traumatic an acknowledgement of our loss and the triumph of those who had taken our place. In the two weeks I spent there on that first visit, I travelled up and down the country of my birth, looking at the remnants of the old Palestine and at what its new occupants had wrought in the years since our flight in 1948. I was barely able to comprehend the changed landscape of what had been an Arab place, its new inhabitants speaking an alien language, their looks a motley assortment of European, Asian, African, and any mixture of these.

It was a momentous journey that had filled me with bitterness and grief. I remember looking down on a night-time Tel Aviv from the windows of the plane taking me back to London and thinking hopelessly, "Flotsam and jetsam, that's what we've become, scattered and divided. There's no room for us or our memories here. And it won't ever be reversed."

As it transpired, I broke my resolve and returned to the same land several times after 1991, and here I was again. The white walls and white-tiled floor of the huge apartment I would be living in stared back at me silently. The man from the United Nations Development

Programme office in Jerusalem, who had driven me to Ramallah, had left—it felt more like abandoned—me with affable expressions of welcome and reassurance that I would be very happy staying there. My footsteps echoed through the wide, tiled hall, the three large bedrooms, and spacious double reception room with its separate seating areas for men and women in the conventional Arab style. I wondered when on earth I would ever be inviting the hordes of people needed to fill them.

*

Like many Palestinians, my greatest pursuit, indeed obsession, for most of my adult life had been Palestine. There was no room in it for much else. I lived and breathed it, worried about its adversities which felt as urgent and immediate as if they were happening beside me. I kept abreast of all its news, read constantly, combed through the internet for more information, monitored the media, talked to other activists, attended and also organised meetings and conferences, and wrote endlessly about it—to such an extent that when anyone asked what I did for a living, I would answer, "I'm a full-time Palestinian!" It was not really true, of course, since I had worked as a doctor of medicine, been a medical historian and later become an academic. But being a Palestinian was the only thing that felt real.

However, after years of activism I had begun to feel disconnected and irrelevant. The gap between what seemed like shadow-fencing with Israel in the security of London and the real fight taking place on the ground in Palestine was too great to ignore. After the Oslo Accords between Israel and the Palestinians were drawn up in 1993, Yasser Arafat and the rest of the leadership returned to Palestinian soil from forty years of exile. And with them, the centre of gravity of the Palestinian cause and the real political action shifted inside. This made the rest of us still promoting the cause outside Palestine feel left behind, like people trying to catch a train that has long departed.

*

For me, return was at the heart of the issue. Without it, the injustice that had blighted our lives for generations would never cease. One day, when my sister and I had been discussing our fragmented family and how dispersed we were, how no one lived close to the other, each alone in the world, and how unnatural it all was, she said bitterly, "If we had never left our country none of this would ever have happened. We would have been amongst our kin, growing up together, helping each other, none of us living or dying alone."

What my time in Palestine had really shown me was that the two fundamentals I had always lived by were transformed out of all recognition. There was no national cause any more, and no unified struggle for return. What future we all had lay with those who lived here, in the West Bank, Gaza and Jerusalem under Israel's occupation, at the mercy of their success or failure to rebuild our cause. And if ever we went back, it would be through them, and no one else.

This is an edited excerpt from Return: A Palestinian Memoir *by Ghada Karmi (republished by Verso Books, 2024).*

SUNDAY NOVEMBER 30

NOVEMBER 30, 1999 The World Trade Organization meeting in Seattle is disrupted by massive anti-globalization protests. "When we smash a window, we aim to destroy the thin veneer of legitimacy that surrounds private property rights." —ACME COLLECTIVE, "ON THE VIOLENCE OF PROPERTY"

DECEMBER 1, 1955 Rosa Parks is arrested for refusing to give up her seat on a segregated bus, which triggers a boycott organized by the Women's Political Council of Montgomery. "Negroes have rights, too, for if Negroes did not ride the busses, they could not operate." —WOMEN'S POLITICAL COUNCIL PAMPHLET

MONDAY DECEMBER 1

DECEMBER 4, 1969 Fred Hampton, Black Panther leader, is assassinated in a raid on his apartment by the Chicago Police with the help of the FBI. "We've got to go up on the mountaintop to make this motherfucker understand, goddamnit, that we are coming from the valley!" —HAMPTON SPEECH AT OLIVET CHURCH

DECEMBER 5, 1978 Wei Jingsheng posts his manifesto "The Fifth Modernization," which was critical of the Communist leadership, to Beijing's Democracy Wall, and is imprisoned for fifteen years. "Let us find out for ourselves what should be done."

TUESDAY DECEMBER 2

DECEMBER 6, 1928 The United Fruit Company violently suppresses a workers' strike in Colombia, in what becomes known as the Banana Massacre.

DECEMBER 6, 2008 Greek police shoot and kill Alexandros Grigoropoulos, a fifteen-year-old boy, sparking three weeks of rioting, protests, and occupations around the country. "We are here we are everywhere we are an image from the future." —OCCUPATION STATEMENT, ATHENS SCHOOL OF ECONOMICS AND BUSINESS STUDENTS

WEDNESDAY DECEMBER 3

Rioters in Athens, 2008

THURSDAY DECEMBER 4

NOTES:

FRIDAY DECEMBER 5

SATURDAY DECEMBER 6

SUNDAY DECEMBER 7

MONDAY DECEMBER 8

TUESDAY DECEMBER 9

DECEMBER 7, 1896 Antonio Maceo, an Afro-Cuban revolutionary, known as the Bronze Titan, dies in the fight for Cuban independence. "Whoever tries to conquer Cuba will gain nothing but the dust of her blood-soaked soil—if he doesn't perish in the struggle first!" —MACEO'S OATH

DECEMBER 9, 2002 To Huu, one of the Viet Minh's most celebrated poets, dies.

"The ditches must go deeper than my hatred.
The work must fly faster than my tears."
—"GUERRILLA WOMAN"

DECEMBER 10, 2008 Charter 08, a document for greater democratization, is published, signed by more than 350 Chinese writers, including poet and essayist Woeser, and human rights activist Liu Xiaobo.

DECEMBER 11, 1977 Moroccan poet Saida Menebhi dies in prison after a thirty-four-day hunger strike. Her work was central in the nationwide attempt to recover the history of the thousands of people who were "disappeared" in the 1970s and 1980s.

"Prison is ugly
you draw it my child
with black marks
for the bars and grills"

DECEMBER 11, 2012 Theresa Spence, chief of Attawapiskat First Nations in Canada, begins a hunger strike that would set off the indigenous sovereignty movement Idle No More.

DECEMBER 13, 1797 Heinrich Heine, German-Jewish poet and essayist, is born. No writer would be more hated by the Nazis.

"Ye fools, so closely to search my trunk!
Ye will find in it really nothing:
My contraband goods I carry about
In my head, not hid in my clothing"
—"A WINTER'S TALE"

WEDNESDAY DECEMBER 10

Protest in Hong Kong against the arrest of Liu Xiaobo, one of the authors of Charter 08

THURSDAY DECEMBER 11

NOTES:

FRIDAY DECEMBER 12

SATURDAY DECEMBER 13

SUNDAY DECEMBER 14

MONDAY DECEMBER 15

TUESDAY DECEMBER 16

DECEMBER 14, 2008 Iraqi journalist Muntadhar al-Zaidi throws his shoe at US president George W. Bush at a press conference. "This is a farewell kiss from the Iraqi people, you dog."

DECEMBER 16, 1656 Radical English Quaker leader James Nayler is arrested for blasphemy after reenacting Christ's entry into Jerusalem by entering Bristol on a donkey.

DECEMBER 17, 1830 Simón Bolívar, nicknamed "El Libertador" for leading Bolivia, Colombia, Ecuador, Panama, Peru, and his native Venezuela to independence from Spain, dies. "If my death will help to end factions and to consolidate the Union, I shall go to my grave in peace." —A PROCLAMATION ISSUED A WEEK BEFORE HIS DEATH

DECEMBER 18, 2010 Demonstrations begin in Tunisia, the day after street vendor Mohamed Bouazizi self-immolated in protest of harassment from officials, setting off what would eventually become the Arab Spring.

DECEMBER 19, 1944 US soldier Kurt Vonnegut becomes a Nazi prisoner of war. The experience later shapes his novels, which often explore anti-authoritarian and anti-war themes. "There is no reason goodness cannot triumph over evil, so long as the angels are as organized as the Mafia." —CAT'S CRADLE

DECEMBER 20, 1986 More than 30,000 students march through Shanghai chanting pro-democracy slogans. "When will the people be in charge?"

WEDNESDAY DECEMBER 17

Demonstrators face police lines on Aveunue Bourguiba, Central Tunis, 2011

THURSDAY DECEMBER 18

NOTES:

FRIDAY DECEMBER 19

SATURDAY DECEMBER 20

SUNDAY DECEMBER 21

MONDAY DECEMBER 22

TUESDAY DECEMBER 23

DECEMBER 23, 1970 After being captured in Bolivia while working as a chronicler for Che Guevara, French journalist Régis Debray is released from prison. "For Che the true difference, the true frontier, is not the one which separates a Bolivian from a Peruvian, a Peruvian from an Argentinian, an Argentinian from a Cuban. It is the one that separates the Latin Americans from the Yankees."
—DEBRAY'S TESTIMONY AT HIS COURT-MARTIAL

DECEMBER 23, 1986 Dissident and Nobel Peace Prize–winner Andrei Sakharov returns to Moscow after six years spent in internal exile for protesting the Soviet war in Afghanistan. "Freedom of thought is the only guarantee against an infection of people by mass myths, which, in the hands of treacherous hypocrites and demagogues, can be transformed into bloody dictatorship."

DECEMBER 25, 1831 Samuel Sharpe, leader of the Native Baptists of Montego Bay, leads Jamaican slaves in the Great Jamaican Slave Revolt, which was instrumental in abolishing chattel slavery. "I would rather die upon yonder gallows than live in slavery." —SHARPE'S LAST WORDS

DECEMBER 25, 1927 B. R. Ambedkar, an architect of the Indian constitution who was born into the Dalit caste of "untouchables," leads followers to burn the Manusmriti, an ancient text justifying the hierarchy. The "untouchables" were relegated to occupations considered impure, like butchering and waste removal.

DECEMBER 25, 1977 Domitila Barrios de Chungara, an activist with the militant Bolivian labor group Housewives' Committee, begins a hunger strike that leads to the end of the US-backed Bolivian dictatorship. "The first battle to be won is to let the woman, the man, the children participate in the struggle of the working class, so that the home can become a stronghold that the enemy can't overcome."

WEDNESDAY DECEMBER 24

B. R. Ambedkar (1891-1956) during his tenure as chairman of the committee for drafting the constitution, 1950

THURSDAY DECEMBER 25

NOTES:

FRIDAY DECEMBER 26

SATURDAY DECEMBER 27

SUNDAY DECEMBER 28

MONDAY DECEMBER 29

TUESDAY DECEMBER 30

DECEMBER 30, 1884 William Morris, Eleanor Marx, and others establish the Socialist League, a revolutionary organization in the UK. "Civilization has reduced the workman to such a skinny and pitiful existence, that he scarcely knows how to frame a desire for any life much better." —MORRIS, *HOW I BECAME A SOCIALIST*

DECEMBER 30, 1896 José Rizal, Filipino nationalist revolutionary and writer, is executed by the Spanish.

DECEMBER 973 Philosopher and poet Abu al-Ala al-Ma'arri, a constant champion of reason against superstition, authority, and tradition, is born near Aleppo, Syria.

"But some hope a divine leader with prophetic voice
Will rise amid the gazing silent ranks
An idle thought! There's none to lead but reason
To point the morning and evening ways."

JANUARY 1, 1970 Gil Scott-Heron, the poet and recording artist who became a voice of black protest culture, releases his album *Small Talk at 125th and Lenox*, whose opening track is "The Revolution Will Not be Televised."

"The revolution will not make you look five pounds thinner,
the revolution will not be televised, Brother."

WEDNESDAY DECEMBER 31

Gil Scott-Heron (1949–2011)

THURSDAY JANUARY 1

NOTES:

FRIDAY JANUARY 2

SATURDAY JANUARY 3

V

VERSO READING LISTS

POLITICAL THEORY

DECOLONIAL MARXISM:
ESSAYS FROM THE PAN-AFRICAN REVOLUTION
WALTER RODNEY

HOW TO BE AN ANTICAPITALIST
IN THE TWENTY-FIRST CENTURY
ERIK OLIN WRIGHT

THE ORIGIN OF CAPITALISM:
A LONGER VIEW
ELLEN MEISKINS WOOD

IMAGINED COMMUNITIES:
REFLECTIONS ON THE ORIGIN AND SPREAD OF
NATIONALISM
BENEDICT ANDERSON

FOR A LEFT POPULISM
CHANTAL MOUFFE

RADICAL HISTORIES

INSURGENT EMPIRE: ANTICOLONIALISM
AND THE MAKING OF BRITISH DISSENT
PRIYAMVADA GOPAL

THE COMMON WIND:
AFRO-AMERICAN CURRENTS IN THE AGE OF THE
HAITIAN REVOLUTION
JULIUS S. SCOTT

SET THE NIGHT ON FIRE:
L.A. IN THE SIXTIES
MIKE DAVIS AND JON WIENER

DARING TO HOPE: MY LIFE IN THE 1970S
SHEILA ROWBOTHAM

BAD GAYS:
A HOMOSEXUAL HISTORY
HUW LEMMEY AND BEN MILLER

THE RECKONING: FROM THE
SECOND SLAVERY TO ABOLITION, 1776–1888
ROBIN BLACKBURN

LINEAGES OF THE ABSOLUTIST STATE
PERRY ANDERSON

PHILOSOPHY AND THEORY

THE FORCE OF NONVIOLENCE:
THE ETHICAL IN THE POLITICAL
JUDITH BUTLER

THE AUTOMATIC FETISH:
THE LAW OF VALUE IN MARX'S CAPITAL
BEVERLEY BEST

CRITIQUE OF EVERYDAY LIFE
HENRI LEFEBVRE

MINIMA MORALIA:
REFLECTIONS FROM DAMAGED LIFE
THEODOR ADORNO

RACE AND ETHNICITY

FUTURES OF BLACK RADICALISM
EDITED BY GAYE THERESA JOHNSON
AND ALEX LUBIN

AISTHESIS: SCENES FROM
THE AESTHETIC REGIME OF ART
JACQUES RANCIÈRE

ECONOMICS

THE NEW SPIRIT OF CAPITALISM
LUC BOLTANSKI AND EVE CHIAPELLO

THE PRODUCTION OF MONEY:
HOW TO BREAK THE POWER OF BANKERS
ANN PETTIFOR

THE COMPLETE WORKS OF ROSA LUXEMBURG,
VOLUME II: ECONOMIC WRITINGS 2
ROSA LUXEMBURG

A COMPANION TO MARX'S CAPITAL,
VOLUME 1 AND VOLUME 2
DAVID HARVEY

FORTUNES OF FEMINISM: FROM STATE-
MANAGED CAPITALISM TO NEOLIBERAL CRISIS
NANCY FRASER

CITIES AND ARCHITECTURE

FEMINIST CITY:
CLAIMING SPACE IN A MAN-MADE WORLD
LESLIE KERN

MUNICIPAL DREAMS:
THE RISE AND FALL OF COUNCIL HOUSING
JOHN BOUGHTON

EXTRASTATECRAFT:
THE POWER OF INFASTRUCTURE SPACE
KELLER EASTERLING

CAPITAL CITY:
GENTRIFICATION AND THE REAL ESTATE STATE
SAMUEL STEIN

REBEL CITIES:
FROM THE RIGHT TO THE CITY
TO THE URBAN REVOLUTION
DAVID HARVEY

ACTIVISM AND RESISTANCE

THE VERSO BOOK OF DISSENT:
REVOLUTIONARY WORDS FROM
THREE MILLENNIA OF REBELLION
AND RESISTANCE
EDITED BY ANDREW HSIAO AND AUDREA LIM

THE END OF POLICING
ALEX S. VITALE

OUR HISTORY IS THE FUTURE:
STANDING ROCK VERSUS THE DAKOTA ACCESS
PIPELINE, AND THE LONG TRADITION OF
INDIGENOUS RESISTANCE
NICK ESTES

DIRECT ACTION:
PROTEST AND THE REINVENTION
OF AMERICAN RADICALISM
L.A. KAUFFMAN

ABOLITION GEOGRAPHY:
ESSAYS TOWARDS LIBERATION
RUTH WILSON GILMORE

FREE PALESTINE

THE PALESTINE LABORATORY:
HOW ISRAEL EXPORTS THE TECHNOLOGY OF
OCCUPATION AROUND THE WORLD
ANTONY LOEWENSTEIN

MURAL
MAHMOUD DARWISH

TEN MYTHS ABOUT ISRAEL
ILAN PAPPE

RETURN: A PALESTINIAN MEMOIR
GHADA KARMI

THE KILLING OF GAZA:
REPORTS ON A CATASTROPHE
GIDEON LEVY

DIARY OF A CRISIS: ISRAEL IN TURMOIL
SAUL FRIEDLÄNDER

NOTES

NOTES

NOTES

NOTES

NOTES

NOTES

NOTES

NOTES

NOTES

NOTES

NOTES